CONTEMPORARY'S
THE WRITE STUFF

Shaping Sentences

Gail Shea

Consultant
Joan Meginniss
Adult Education Coordinator
College of Lake County
Grayslake, Illinois

Coordinator of Field Testing
Charles Nystrom
ABE/GED Instructor
Lake Shore Education Center
Waukegan, Illinois

Project Editor
Ellen Carley Frechette

Editorial Director
Caren Van Slyke

CB
CONTEMPORARY
BOOKS
CHICAGO

Published by Contemporary Books, Inc.
180 North Michigan Avenue, Chicago, Illinois 60601
Manufactured in the United States of America
International Standard Book Number: 0-8092-5205-8

Published simultaneously in Canada by
Fitzhenry & Whiteside
91 Granton Drive
Richmond Hill, Ontario L4B 2N5
Canada

Copy Editor
Christine M. Benton

Editorial Assistant
Julie Landau

Production Editor
Patricia Reid

Art and Illustration
Princess Louise El
Arvid Carlson
Ellen Berry

Illustrations
Michael Shea

Cover Design
Georgene Sainati

Cover photograph © Chuck O'Rear, WestLight
Inset photograph by C. C. Cain Photography

Table of Contents

Section III: Repairing

An Answer Sampler

Acknowledgments

Ernest Hemingway, excerpted from *The Old Man and The Sea*. Copyright © 1952 by Ernest Hemingway; copyright renewed 1980 by Mary Hemingway. Reprinted with the permission of Charles Scribner's Sons.

Excerpt from "I Have a Dream," reprinted by permission of Joan Daves. Copyright © 1963 by Martin Luther King, Jr.

Excerpts from speech by Geraldine Ferraro. Presented at the 1984 National Democratic Convention in acceptance of the Vice-Presidential nomination of the Democratic party. Reprinted with the permission of Geraldine Ferraro.

This book is dedicated to the memory of Mary P. Shea.

Notes to the Instructor

Many people are reluctant to start writing because they know they will make mistakes in grammar and spelling. They are afraid that everything they put on paper is final and that they should somehow be able to write perfectly the first time around. They view writing not as a means of expression but as an exercise in comma placement and verb tenses. Such concerns prevent these people from ever getting started writing.

Shaping Sentences helps students get over this hurdle. By starting off with the transition from speech to writing, the book helps to take the "mystery" out of writing. In the first chapter, students are encouraged to write the way they speak—to get their ideas onto paper. Subsequent chapters assist students in improving their language so that it can easily be understood by readers. By understanding this *process of writing*, students can see that their ideas are every bit as important as punctuation and spelling, and they will be less reluctant to write.

Although *Shaping Sentences* deals with the building and combining of ideas at the sentence level, students do not simply practice writing isolated and disconnected sentences. Instead, notice that many of the activities in the book require a series of sentences all related to the same topic. This is done in an effort to emphasize to students that a sentence rarely exists on its own. It is usually a part of a longer form of communication, such as a paragraph, letter, or essay. Writing a series of related rather than isolated sentences is more meaningful for any writer, including the beginning one.

Shaping Sentences can be used as an introductory writing book or as a companion to the other books in *The Write Stuff* series, *Putting It in Paragraphs* and *Writing for a Purpose*. When your students have worked through this text, they will have developed the ability to use a variety of sentence patterns. More importantly, they will have developed confidence in their ability to write.

Section I:

Inventing

Chapter 1

Introducing Sentences

─────── **Your Chapter Goals Are** ───────

1. to form simple sentences from real-life situations.

2. to see how different types of sentences are used for special purposes.

3. to learn how to write basic action sentences.

We create sentences to communicate with other people. First, we observe certain things in the world. We observe by seeing, smelling, touching, tasting, and hearing. We use words for what we observe. We string these words together to talk or write in sentences. Writing or talking is like thinking out loud so that others can understand.

Good writers work to sharpen their senses. They also work on their ability to use words. Good writers know how to use their ability to speak and think to become better writers. This chapter will help you use the abilities that you already have to become a better writer.

Sentences in Real Life

——— Setting Your Thoughts Spinning ———

Do you use sentences when you talk? Do other people? Listen to a conversation and see for yourself.

One evening, two young mothers were riding home on a city bus. Each had her little girl sitting near her. Their conversation began like this:

First Mother:	"Where are you headed?"
Second Mother:	"Visiting my folks."
First Mother:	"How old's your little girl?"
Second Mother:	"Melissa's three."
First Mother:	"They're the same age then. Carrie is three, too."
Second Mother:	"Does Carrie go to preschool?"
First Mother:	"Rutley Preschool."
Second Mother:	"Why Rutley?"
First Mother:	"Because it's close to home."

Did these women speak in sentences? Did they use sentences all of the time or some of the time?

——————— Pulling It All Together ———————

People begin using sentences at a very young age. As we grow, we string words together in many different ways. You already know the basic sentence patterns of English, and you use them often when you speak.

In many ways, writing is talk put on paper. We speak in sentences, so we write in sentences as well. However, we do not speak in sentences all of the time. We can shortcut. Our faces and hands help our words with looks and gestures.

For instance, if a fisherman wants to talk about the fish he caught, he says "It was this big." Then he uses his hands to show how big. In a letter, however, he would have to write down the size. "I caught a fish sixteen inches long." His reader is able to understand through words only.

When we write, the way we form sentences becomes more important. Clear, well-written sentences help the reader understand what we are saying.

———— Working Out ————

We feel comfortable with sentences when we talk. See for yourself how easy it is to write the way you talk. Make up a conversation that the two women on the bus could have had. Have them talk about __ONE__ of the following topics.

1. taking their children to get their shots

2. whom they voted for in the last presidential election

3. how bad the bus service has been

Fill in the lines below with your conversation.

First Mother: "_____

_____"

Second Mother: "_____

_____"

First Mother: "_____

_____"

Second Mother: "_____

_____"

First Mother: "_____

_____"

Second Mother: "_____

_____"

First Mother: "_____

_____"

A SAMPLE CONVERSATION IS ON PAGE 162.

———— Trick of the Trade ————

Writers sometimes keep notebooks. These can be very helpful. You can write about things you see or think about. You can also write down words you hear but don't know the meaning of. Then you can look up these words in a dictionary later. You can also write down sentences you may want to use later in a letter or story. Catchy words or phrases you want to remember (like "Where's the beef?") can be written down as well. Try using a notebook. A small one that could fit into your pocket or purse will do. Refer to the notebook when you write.

Sentences for Purposes

——— Setting Your Thoughts Spinning ———

Are there different kinds of sentences? Do we change the way we string words together to suit our purposes? The "word strings" below are scrambled. Unscramble them and write them as sentences. Think about why you would use each sentence.

son dinner late for home came my.

_____

not dinner late do home come for.

_____

did late home for come you why dinner?

_____

late always you for come dinner home!

_____

——————— Pulling It All Together ———————

We have reasons for speaking with others. Mostly we want to get or give something. We may want to get a job from someone or get someone to do something for us. At times we may just want to get information. We also use language to give information and to give of our emotions.

We change the order of words to show different purposes. The four basic purposes for sentences are explained below.

1. TELLING OR GIVING INFORMATION: When we tell someone something, our voices start out even, stay even, and then drop off at the end to a stop. When we write telling sentences, we begin with a capital letter and end with a period.

Say this telling sentence out loud. Notice how your voice drops.

Marsha bought a new blender from Sears.

2. ASKING QUESTIONS: When we ask a question, our voices end on a slightly rising question note. The question mark stands for this note when we write.

Say this question out loud. Notice what your voice does.

Did Marsha buy a new blender from Sears?

3. GIVING COMMANDS OR INSTRUCTIONS: At times, we need to tell people what to do. We tell a person what action to take and often do not even mention his or her name. Our voices stay even or get louder with instructions or commands. When written, commands end with periods or exclamation marks (!).

Say these commands out loud. Say the first one in your usual voice. Say the one with the exclamation mark more strongly.

Take a left on Dearborn Street.

Leave me alone!

4. SHOWING STRONG FEELING: Our tone of voice fits our emotions when we talk. To show strong feeling when we write, we use an exclamation mark.

Say this sentence out loud. Say it with feeling.

That movie was just wonderful!

———————— Working Out ————————

Part A

Match the kinds of sentences in the first column to the purposes in the second column.

1. Telling   **a.** to give an order or instructions

2. Question   **b.** to give information

3. Command   **c.** to show emotion

4. Feeling   **d.** to get information (ask)

Part B

Below, four situations are described. Any of these could have happened to you. Read about each situation. Then write what you would have said in the situation.

Did you have a reason for saying that? Write the main purpose for what you said on the line under your sentence. Your purpose should be (1) to give information, (2) to ask a question, (3) to give a command, or (4) to show emotion. Remember that there is no one correct answer. Whatever <u>you</u> would say is what you should write.

1. You are in the dentist's chair. The dentist has just given you a shot of novocaine. She asks you how your mouth feels.

   What would you say? *It feels funny.*

   Your main purpose was to *give information.*

Now you. What would you say?_____

_____

Your main purpose was to _____

2. You are sitting at the dinner table in your mother-in-law's house. You could use some salt and pepper on your potatoes. The shakers are across the table out of your reach.

What would you say?_____

_____

Your main purpose was to _____

3. It has stopped raining. You have a child with you. This child cannot wait to go out and play. You're worried that the child will get dirty.

What would you say? _____

_____

Your main purpose was to _____

4. The bus fare just went up. You have no idea what it is. You get on the bus and look at the driver.

What would you say? _____

_____

Your main purpose was to _____

Part C

Get used to changing the order of words when you write. For example, certain question words can be moved to the front of a sentence to make a command or question.

You are taking a later train.

Are you taking a later train?

Take a later train.

You can always change words around to suit your purpose. Look at the telling sentences below. Rewrite each—first as a question and then as a command or an instruction.

1. The dentist gave me a shot of novocaine.

QUESTION:

COMMAND:

2. I would like the salt and pepper.

QUESTION:

COMMAND:

3. You are getting ready to go.

QUESTION:

COMMAND:

4. You are going to get on this bus.

QUESTION:

COMMAND:

5. You understand that we love you.

QUESTION:

COMMAND:

SAMPLE ANSWERS ARE ON PAGES 162-63.

On Your Own

Choose ONE of the following activities. You may want to do a little thinking before you write.

Watch a soap opera or read a romantic story in a magazine. These may give you ideas of things to write in the first activity below.

1. Write a conversation (about twelve lines long) between two lovers that are breaking up. Try to use telling sentences, questions, commands, and strong feeling sentences in the conversation.

If you choose the next activity, a police show on TV or a newspaper article might give you ideas to include in your conversation.

2. Someone has dented a man's car fender in a parking lot. Write a conversation (about twelve lines long) that might take place between the man and the driver who dented the car. Try to use telling sentences, questions, commands or instructions, and strong emotion sentences in your conversation.

What Makes a Sentence?

——— Setting Your Thoughts Spinning ———

Are these sentences?

1. Visiting my folks.
2. Rutley Preschool.

——————— Pulling It All Together ———————

The expressions above are from the conversation on page 4 between the two two women on the bus. Look back at this conversation. From the conversation, you know what the women meant when they said these things. However, just because you know what they mean does not mean that they are sentences.

When we write something other than a conversation, we should always use complete sentences. Complete sentences help the reader follow what we are saying. Look at expression 2 above. Is this a complete sentence? Would this group of words mean anything if it were on its own? A reader probably would look at these words and say, "What about Rutley Preschool? What do you want to say about it?"

This group of words is not a sentence because it does not have a verb. A **verb** tells the reader what is happening in the sentence. For example, the verbs in the following sentences are in dark type.

Rutley Preschool **closes** at 3:30 P.M.

Rutley Preschool **has** a library.

Verbs that tell what someone or something is doing are called **action verbs**. These are words like *close, fall, love, hate, think, dream*. Action verbs are anything we can do. In the next chapter, you'll learn about another kind of verb, the **being verb.** For now, let's concentrate on actions. Underline the actions, or verbs, in the following sentences.

1. Lorenzo jogs every day.
2. The wind whistled and howled through the trees.

As you can see from the last example, sentences can have more than one verb. Both *whistled* and *howled* are the verbs.

In addition to having verbs, complete sentences have **subjects.** A subject tells you who or what is performing the action in the sentence. Look at expression 1 above. You now know that this is not a complete sentence because it does not tell you *who* or *what* is *visiting my folks*.

In the sentences below, the subjects are in dark type.

We are visiting my folks.

The exhausted **workers** walked slowly home.

Can you see that each dark type word tells you who or what is doing the action in the sentence? Now go back to the two sentences where you underlined the verbs. Circle the subject of each sentence. Ask yourself, "Who jogs? What whistled and howled?"

You now know that a sentence must have at least two things:

  1. a verb.

  2. a subject.

Now you'll have a chance to practice making sentences.

———— Working Out ————

The following groups of words are not complete sentences. Each one is missing either a subject or a verb. In order to make each sentence complete, add the element that is missing. The questions after each group of words should help you decide what to write. The first one is done for you.

1. A very tall woman.   *(What did she do?)*

   A very tall woman entered the beauty shop.

2. Spoke quietly to the manager.   *(Who spoke to the manager?)*

   _____

3. Had long black hair and wore
   heavy eye makeup.   *(Who had long hair?)*

   _____

4. The elderly manager.   *(What did he do?)*

   _____

5. Was sitting behind a white
   screen.   *(Who was sitting?)*

   _____

6. Angry and annoyed, he.   *(What did he do?)*

   _____

7. Finally, the two people.   *(What did they do?)*

   _____

8. Laughed about it later.   *(Who laughed?)*

   _____

SAMPLE ANSWERS ARE ON PAGE 163.

Complete Thought

———— Setting Your Thoughts Spinning ————

Are these sentences?

> Because it's close to home.
>
> While I sat on the subway.

They both have subjects and verbs, don't they?

———————— Pulling It All Together ————————

If someone walked up to you and said, "Because it's close to home," wouldn't you want to say "Well, finish what you're saying?" You would probably want to know more about what was close to home and what happened as a result.

You would also probably have lots of questions if someone said, "While I sat on the subway." What happened while you were on the subway? Did you get robbed? Did you read a newspaper? In short, you would want to have more information.

To be complete, a sentence must do more than have a subject and a verb. A sentence must be a **complete thought**. In other words, a writer must give the reader some new information in each sentence. The sentence must mean something <u>on its own</u>. For example, the following groups of words are now complete sentences. Your readers will be satisfied because they are not left hanging.

> Melissa goes to Rutley Preschool because it's close to home.
>
> While I sat on the subway, I saw an old friend.

Can you see that these sentences give you some new information? They are complete sentences because they can stand on their own.

Which of the following is a complete sentence? Both have a subject and a verb, but one is not a complete thought.

> I looked away when I saw her coming.
>
> When I saw her coming.

Can you see that the first sentence gives you some new information? Do you also see that the second group of words leaves you hanging?

— Working Out —

Each of the following groups of words has a subject and a verb. However, each one is not a sentence because it does not express a complete thought. Make each group of words a complete sentence by adding an idea to help the sentence stand on its own. Write the complete sentence on the line provided. The first one is done for you.

1. After we watched the baseball game.

   After we watched the baseball game, we went out for pizza.

2. So that they would not be late.

   _____

   _____

3. If my boss would just leave me alone.

   _____

   _____

4. When Kingsford saw them coming.

   _____

   _____

5. Before the sun went down.

   _____

   _____

6. Because he needed the money.

   _____

   _____

7. After Dawn took the test.

   _____

   _____

8. Since we all like sausages.

   _____

   _____

SAMPLE ANSWERS ARE ON PAGE 163.

Putting More Action in Your Sentences

——— Setting Your Thoughts Spinning ———

Do you sometimes find yourself using the same action words over and over again? Words like *walk*, *look*, *say*, and others can tell your reader about an action. However, because they are often overused, they become boring. What words can be used in their place?

——— Pulling It All Together ———

An activity called **brainstorming** can often help you think of useful words and phrases for your writing. If you find yourself using the same words over and over again, take some time to brainstorm for new ideas.

For example, write the word *talk* on a piece of paper. Now think of all different kinds of "talking" and write them down underneath. Don't worry about whether they are good ideas right now. Write down everything you can think of. Here's an example of one writer's brainstorm list.

Talk			
converse	chat	gab	speak
address	confer	utter	express
gossip	discuss		

Each of these words means something a little bit different. Say each one to yourself and get a feeling for what it means to you. You can see that you probably would use each word differently. Read the paragraph below and notice how boring it is when the same action word is repeated. Rewrite the paragraph below, replacing the dark-type words. Use as many different words as possible.

> As they waited in line for the movie, people spent their time **talking.** Women from the neighborhood **talked** about who was seeing whom and what was on TV that night. Young children **talked** noisily to each other, while the older men quietly **talked.** A policeman **talked about** politics with a newspaper reporter.

Now read your paragraph over. Don't the actions stand out a lot more? You probably noticed that the new sentences are more interesting to read. By replacing tired, overused words, you have given your reader a better picture.

Working Out

Look at the picture of a rescue taking place. On a separate sheet of paper, write down all the different actions you see taking place. Include other actions that happen at a rescue scene if you'd like. If you have trouble thinking of new action words, try brainstorming to come up with new words. Next, use these action verbs to describe the scene. Try to write at least six sentences and use variety in your writing.

A SAMPLE PARAGRAPH IS ON PAGE 164.

Trick of the Trade

Brainstorming helps when thinking of new words, but sometimes writers need help coming up with "just the right word." A book called a **thesaurus** can help. A thesaurus lists both synonyms (words that mean almost the same thing) and antonyms (words that mean the opposite). A simple one is *Roget's Thesaurus in Dictionary Form*. It comes in paperback. Make sure you get the one that says *in Dictionary Form* in the title.

Describing the Action

———— Setting Your Thoughts Spinning ————

You just learned that action sentences have a subject and an action verb. Is this all there is to an action sentence? Which group of sentences below gives you a better idea of what is happening?

The guard left his feet. He cocked his arm back and let the ball go. A hand shot up. A referee's whistle cracked the air, ending play. The ball sailed through the hoop.

The guard swiftly left his feet. Urgently, he cocked his arm back and quickly let the ball go. Suddenly, a hand shot up. The referee's whistle loudly cracked the air, ending play. The ball sailed gracefully through the hoop.

———— Pulling It All Together ————

Often, it is not enough to tell our readers just an action and who is performing the action. Our readers may want to know more about what is happening. The second group of sentences above lets us know more about what the basketball players were doing. The guard did not cock his arm back *casually*. He did it *urgently*. A hand did not shoot up *gradually*—it shot up *suddenly*.

Our readers need to know when, where, and how something is being done. Words that help show when, where, and how are called **adverbs** and are discussed below.

Many words or groups of words can tell us **when** something took place. These are words like *tomorrow*, *often*, and *lately*. We add these words to our sentences if we think the information would help the reader understand what we mean. Notice that each group of dark-type words answers the question "when?"

The new color television set will be delivered **tomorrow**.
(<u>When</u> *will the television set be delivered?*)

José's surprise party begins **soon**.
(<u>When</u> *does José's party begin?*)

Sometimes our readers need to know **where** an action is taking place. As writers, we may want to identify something by its location. Notice that the dark-type word answers the question "where?"

Herman looked **down** at his feet.
(<u>Where did Herman look?</u>)

"How" words give the reader more information about an action itself. They tell the reader **how** action was performed. Notice that each dark-type word below answers the question "how?"

> The hockey player came down **hard** on the ice.
> (*How did the player come down?*)

> **Slowly**, the elevator doors began to open.
> (*How did the elevator doors open?*)

These "how" words can also be described. For instance, a door can open *slowly*, or it can open *very slowly*. A model can walk *elegantly* or she can walk *quite elegantly*.

━━━━━━━━━━━━━━━━━ Working Out ━━━━━━━━━━━━━━━━━

Provide "when," "where," and "how" words for the description below.

The scene at the pub last night was really wild. A stranger

_____ walked in and _____ ordered a beer.
　　　how　　　　　　　　　　　　　　*when*

_____, the regular customers realized that they had seen
　　　when

the man _____. He was the one who had gotten into a fight
　　　　　　　when

_____ at Nell's Disco the other night. They looked at him
　　　where

_____ and then _____ asked him to leave.
　　　how　　　　　　　　　　　*how*

_____, a huge brawl broke out _____ in the
　　　when　　　　　　　　　　　　　　　*where*

place. _____ the police arrived and _____
　　　　　when　　　　　　　　　　　　　　*how*

broke up the fight.

ONE POSSIBLE DESCRIPTION IS ON PAGE 164.

Closing the Chapter

──────── You Have Learned That ────────

1. you already know a great deal about sentences from your daily life.

2. different kinds of sentences are used for different purposes.

3. you can use and combine different words called **adverbs** to describe action in your sentences.

──────── An Action Assignment ────────

Did you ever have to leave a note to tell someone how to do something? For instance, did you ever need to leave a note for the repairman or baby-sitter?

Write a note on one of the following topics. Make sure you tell the reader when, where, and how you want something.

1. Write a note to your baby-sitter telling how to fix the dinner you left.

2. Leave a note for a repairman telling him what to fix in your apartment.

3. Write a note to a delivery person to tell her where to leave things while you are on vacation.

Chapter 2

A Chance to Describe Something

1. to see how sentences are used to describe things.

2. to learn about "being" verbs and describing words.

3. to help put more detail in your writing.

Keep your notebook handy. You're going to learn about details. **Details** are all the little things you notice about something. For instance, look at the door to your house or apartment. It may be made of wood. It isn't made of one big piece of wood but of five pieces of pine. It is painted green, but the paint is starting to crack and peel. The doorknob is brown on the outside and gold on the inside. The colors, the kind of wood, and the cracking, peeling paint are all <u>details</u>.

Details tell us the color, shape, and size of something. They can also tell us how much, how often, and what time. If you want to write about something, look at the details. Record these in your notebook.

Sentences that Describe

——— Setting Your Thoughts Spinning ———

Do sentences always show action? Are the groups of words below sentences even though they do not show action?

> He was a great athlete.
>
> The stew tastes good.
>
> Her flowers are beautiful.

——— Pulling It All Together ———

Some sentences do not tell about an action. These sentences are called **describing sentences**. As with action sentences, these describing sentences have subjects and verbs. However, in describing sentences, the subject is not doing an action. The subject is being described.

The verbs in describing sentences are different from action verbs. The most common group of these verbs is called **being verbs**. They are:

> am   is   are
>
> was   were
>
> be   been

Some sentences using these verbs to make descriptions are:

> The front porch **is** clean now.
>
> Rafer Johnson **was** a great athlete.

Sometimes being verbs are used to help action verbs. Don't confuse these with being verbs used to describe. For example:

> Jack **is leaving** for home now.
> (*is leaving* is an action)
>
> Her plane **was taking off** at 7:00.
> (*was taking off* is an action)

Besides being verbs, there are other verbs that can help describe:

> appear   look   sound   become
>
> grow   smell   feel   seem   taste

Some sentences using these verbs are:

> Jaime **appeared** rather angry at the meeting.
>
> The witness's testimony **became** clear to me.
>
> I **feel** better today.

Can you see that there are really no actions taking place in these sentences? The verbs just help the rest of the sentence to describe the subject.

Sometimes, however, the verbs above can be used as action verbs. For example:

> I **looked** for my watch under the couch. *(action)*
>
> I **look** good in blue. *(being)*
>
> The infant **was feeling** her way across the carpet. *(action)*
>
> My son **was feeling** ill this morning. *(being)*

It is important to be able to tell the difference between a being verb and an action verb because we use different kinds of words to describe them. Words that Describe in Chapter 10 will give you more information about these words.

———————— Working Out ————————

Practice deciding whether the underlined verb is a being verb or an action verb. Remember, a being verb helps describe the subject, and an action verb tells you what the subject is doing. Write either *description* or *action* on the space provided. The first one is done for you.

1. That <u>felt</u> good. *description*

2. The blind man <u>felt</u> his way to his seat. _____

3. Shawn <u>was</u> here yesterday. _____

4. Maria <u>was leaving</u> on Thursday. _____

5. I <u>smell</u> a rat. _____

6. Your cherry pie <u>smells</u> terrific. _____

7. Lynn <u>seemed</u> calm. _____

8. The band <u>is playing</u> at the Pepper Club this week.

_____

ANSWERS ARE ON PAGE 164.

Writing Sentences that Describe

——— Setting Your Thoughts Spinning ———

You've probably already noticed that describing sentences have more than a subject and a being verb. Think of other types of words that you use when describing someone or something.

——————— Pulling It All Together ———————

What is different about these two sentences?

> Jo Schwartz was a teacher.

> Jo Schwartz was helpful to us.

Both sentences describe Jo Schwartz, but each does it in its own way. The first sentence uses a **noun** (*teacher*) to describe her. You may remember from grammar lessons that a **noun** is a person, place, or thing. This noun tells us what the subject is.

The second sentence uses a **describing word**, or **adjective**, to tell more about her. This kind of sentence tells us what qualities the subject has. *Helpful* tells us one quality that Jo Schwartz has.

Of course, you can use two or more nouns or describing words after a being verb. For example:

> Jeffrey and his wife were **tired** and **late** for the party.
> (*Tired* and *late* describe *Jeffrey and his wife.*)

> That man is Harry's **boss**, **friend**, and **neighbor**.
> (*Boss, friend,* and *neighbor* tell you what the man is.)

However, don't mix describing words and nouns after a being verb.

> **Wrong:** My father is a **volunteer fireman** and **funny**.
>   (*noun and adjective after being verb*)

> **Right:** My father is a **volunteer fireman** and a **cabdriver**.
>   (*two nouns after being verb*)

> **Right**: My father is **funny** and **friendly**.
>   (*two adjectives after being verb*)

Working Out

Often, we write because we want to describe someone or something to others. Now you have a chance to describe your favorite or least favorite music.

In your notebook or on a separate piece of paper, write about the singers, bands, or kinds of music you like or don't like. The sentence-building chart below organizes the words according to categories. Use the chart to help you put words and ideas together.

Choose a noun, then a being verb, then other nouns or describing words to make up a sentence. Feel free to use your own words as well. If your favorite music or musician is not on the ladder, go ahead and add it in the space provided. You may also use action sentences if you need to.

Nouns	The Jacksons Barbara Mandrell
	Frank Sinatra Elvis Presley
	Bruce Springsteen The Temptations
	The Oak Ridge Boys Tina Turner
	Stevie Wonder
	_____ _____
	radio singer rock group band guitar
	drums bass tune voice beat
	albums rhythm and blues gospel
	country rock and roll jazz
	punk rock pop music
Being Verbs	is are was were have been has
	been remain will be appear
	look sound seem became
Describing	awful moody loud popular stale
	energetic fantastic good average
	entertaining hard beautiful soft old
	boring new sad exciting long

_____

_____

_____

_____

_____

_____

_____

A PARAGRAPH BASED ON THIS CHART CAN BE FOUND ON PAGE 164.

Nouns and Describing Words

——— Setting Your Thoughts Spinning ———

Which paragraph describes the picture better?

The church stood in the courtyard. Its shadow provided the only shade. A wind whipped sand around the courtyard and swayed the bell in the tower. The shadows grew longer. The sun had finally begun to set.

The old adobe church stood in the dusty courtyard. Its lengthening shadow provided the only cool shade. A playful wind whipped soft sand around the empty courtyard and swayed the small bell in the church tower. The dark shadows grew longer. The sweltering sun had finally begun to set.

———————— Pulling It All Together ————————

Notice how the second paragraph has more detail. The church isn't just any church. It is an *old, adobe* church. *Old* and *adobe* are describing words. They are placed in front of the word *church* to help describe that part of the sentence.

When you write a sentence, look at it carefully. See where describing words can be added. It is not enough just to name something. You have to make sure your readers get the right picture in their heads. To your readers, the word church could have meant a *brand-new, stone* church on a city street. It could have meant a *wooden country* church. Without a photograph, the first paragraph might not have given the reader the right picture.

Describing words tell us three things about nouns. First, they can tell us the qualities someone or something may have. For example:

The **old, adobe** church stood in the dusty courtyard.

The driver, **tense** and **exhausted,** pulled off the road.

Second, describing words can tell us whom or what something belongs to.

Phil's jacket fell on the floor.

His neighbor borrowed my motorcycle.

Third, describing words can also tell us amounts.

Rosalind sold **fifty** bumper stickers.

There are only a **few** tickets left at the box office.

Take a **little** stew.

Learn to check your sentences for the detail your reader needs. Find the nouns in your sentences. Think about whether your reader would need to know more about each noun. Does he need to know the qualities of something? What about the number or amount? Also, does your reader need to know whom something belongs to?

———————————— Working Out ————————————

Part A

Describing words make our writing more interesting. First, read the paragraph below and notice how dull and lifeless it sounds. Next, add describing words in the blanks provided on the next page and see how much more detail you can give your reader. Read your improved piece aloud to see how much better it sounds.

Last night I turned my television set to the news. It was time for the weather report. A weatherman was doing the report this time. He said a blizzard was expected. Our city would get snow? I couldn't believe it. We have already had a winter. Next year I'm moving to Florida.

Last night I turned my _____ television set to the

_____ news. It was time for the weather report. A

_____ weatherman was doing the report this time. He

said a _____ blizzard was expected. Our

_____ city would get _____ of snow?

I couldn't believe it. We have already had a _____ winter.

Next year I'm moving to _____ Florida.

Part B

Sometimes writers use a separate sentence for each detail. The result is a lot of short, choppy sentences. Often describing words from one sentence could be added to another sentence. The following exercise will show you how this works.

Read this list of sentences. Combine them by putting describing words (in dark type) next to the words to which they apply. The first few are done for you.

1. Carla works for an answering service.
2. It operates **twenty four hours**.
3. She works the night shift.
4. The night shift is **long and boring**.
5. The building is deserted.
6. The building is **creaky and old**.
7. One night she had quite an experience.
8. It was a **frightening** experience.
9. First she heard the elevator doors open.
10. The elevator doors are **squeaky**.

11. Then she heard footsteps.
12. They were **loud** footsteps.
15. Carla grabbed a paperweight.
16. The paperweight was **heavy and marble**.
17. She ran for the door.
18. The door was **open**.
19. Whack! She looked down at the body on the floor.
20. It was her **boyfriend's** body.
21. The body was **unconscious**.

Carla works for a twenty-four hour answering service. She works the long and boring night shift. The building, creaky and old, is deserted.

_____

_____

_____

SAMPLE ANSWERS ARE ON PAGE 165.

On Your Own

Part A

You would like to write a mystery story. First you must describe the suspects and the scene of a murder. By filling in the blanks below with labels and describing words, you will be able to set the scene for your reader. The first one is filled in for you.

SUSPECTS

Something wasn't *right* _____ about this case. The

_____ butler seemed _____. The other

_____ suspects were _____ also. Mrs.

Reynolds's brother sounded _____, and the

_____ maid looked _____. Could these

_____ people have known more than they were telling?

I told them all to meet me in the _____ library. The

victim's _____ boyfriend was already waiting for us there.

He had been _____ from the start.

SETTING

The old, _____ mansion must have been

_____. Everything rattled. _____ lights flashed

on and off. The _____ wind sounded _____.

The staircase was _____, and the furniture was

_____ and _____. Through the

_____ windows the _____ sky looked

_____.

Part B

Describe the detective in this murder case. Picture what he or she looks like in your own mind and try to get this idea across to your reader. Use describing words and labels wherever you can.

Describing Yourself

——— Setting Your Thoughts Spinning ———

Sometimes we want to let other people know what we are like. We may use the qualities or descriptions of the signs of the zodiac to talk about ourselves.

——— Pulling It All Together ———

How would you describe yourself? What if you had to write about yourself for a company newsletter? How would you describe yourself to a soldier overseas or to someone you wanted to date?

The purpose of this exercise is for you to practice describing things. For fun, you will use signs of the zodiac to describe yourself.

——— Working Out ———

Astrologers are people who study how the stars and planets affect our lives. They believe that the month and day you were born can tell a lot about what you are like as a person. If you don't already know what sign you are, find your birthday on the list below. Your sign is given there.

Aries—March 21 to April 20
Taurus—April 21 to May 20
Gemini—May 21 to June 21
Cancer—June 22 to July 22
Leo—July 23 to August 22
Virgo—August 23 to September 22
Libra—September 23 to October 22
Scorpio—October 23 to November 21
Sagittarius—November 22 to December 20
Capricorn—December 21 to January 19
Aquarius—January 20 to February 18
Pisces—February 19 to March 20

Now find your sign below. Look at the qualities and describing words next to your sign. Do any of these sound like you? Use these words to help you write a ten-line description of yourself. If these words do not describe you, say so! Then use other words that sound more like you. Use the being verbs listed below to help you write good describing sentences.

For example, here are two sentences that a person wrote to describe herself:

I am a Virgo, but I am not **selfish** or **conceited.** I
   think I am pretty **generous**.

Aries, Leo, Sagittarius	active lively spirited vigorous powerful energetic ambitious excitable
Taurus, Virgo, Capricorn	practical obedient determined firm stubborn hardworking selfish conceited rich intense
Gemini, Libra, Aquarius	intelligent smooth diligent adaptable wise talkative loud kind interesting
Cancer, Scorpio, Pisces	sensitive emotional imaginative inconsistent flexible responsive active caring strong
Being Verbs	am was have been will be

A DESCRIPTION BASED ON THIS CHART
CAN BE FOUND ON PAGE 165.

Closing the Chapter

———— You Have Learned ————

1. that there are verbs we use to set up descriptions. These are called **being verbs**.

2. that there are certain words we use to describe qualities, ownership, or amount. These words are called **adjectives**.

3. that writers should try to give the reader as much detail as possible.

———— One More Chance to Describe Someone ————

The place where you work has a newsletter. Write a description of your boss for this newsletter. Talk about the qualities he or she has for being a good boss. Describe your boss's work habits or office, if you'd like. If you don't have a boss or supervisor, describe one that you would like to have.

Chapter 3
Timing Your Sentences

—————— Your Chapter Goals Are ——————

1. to see how verbs show time in sentences.

2. to learn to use the right verb for your writing purposes.

3. to learn to use time words in your sentences.

The Hopi Indians have no present tense in their language. That is, they have no verbs that show that something is happening right now. They have no verbs like *watch*, *talks*, *is*, or *are*. You might say something like "Jack is on his way over." However, a Hopi Indian would not use his language in that way.

To a Hopi Indian, once something is started, it is already becoming part of the past. If something hasn't happened yet, then it belongs to the future. To write like a Hopi Indian, you might say, "Jack left. He will arrive soon," instead of "Jack is on his way over."

We use different verb tenses and time words according to what we want to say. Do you want to write about something that happened in the past, something that is going on now, or something that has not happened yet? We have different forms of verbs for those different times.

The Time Is Now

——— Setting Your Thoughts Spinning ———

People who speak English have their own way of showing time in sentences. We do not use the same method as the Hopi Indians do. How many times do the following sentences show?

> Everyone votes on the first Tuesday in November.
>
> We are voting with punch cards in this precinct.
>
> Jessie will vote after work.
>
> I voted for our governor in the last election.

——————— Pulling It All Together ———————

Three different times are being shown in these sentences. In this chapter, we will learn about how the verb in a sentence shows these times: the **present**, **past**, or **future tense**. First let's concentrate on the present tense.

There are two forms of the present tense. The first shows what is happening now. For example:

> LaTasha **is wearing** yellow today.
>
> The buildings **are** still **burning**.

Each of these sentences is telling about something that is taking place <u>now</u>. The verbs of the sentences tell us this. Notice that each present tense uses the *ing* form of the verb (*wearing, burning*.) Also notice that a form of being verb is also needed (*am, is,* or *are.*)

The second form of the present is used to show that something happens all the time, or "as a rule." For example:

> We **vote** on the first Tuesday in November.
>
> The Great Sale **starts** on the first Sunday of the month.
>
> Halley's Comet **comes** back every seventy-five years.

Can you see that each of these sentences tells something that happens regularly or is always true?

Notice that some forms of this present tense have an *s* on the end and some do not. Writers sometimes get confused over whether an *s* is needed in the present. Here is an easy way to decide:

> If the subject of the verb is *one* person, place, or thing (but not *I* or *you*), put an *s* on the end of the present tense verb.

—————— Working Out ——————

In this exercise, get used to using both forms of the present tense. First underline the present tense verb in the sentence. Then, on the line provided, rewrite the sentence using the other present tense form. The first is done for you.

1. Cynthia <u>goes</u> to Erie for her medical exam.

   Cynthia is going to Erie for her medical exam.

2. The mail is taking a long time to get here!

   _____

3. We use the expressway to get to work.

   _____

4. Hank enjoys his new Cadillac more than ever.

   _____

5. I am learning all kinds of new skills at work.

   _____

6. Jesse is looking really sharp these days.

   _____

7. As usual, the race is ending before midnight.

   _____

8. You try very hard on tests, Bill.

   _____

ANSWERS ARE ON PAGE 165.

Moving Through Time

——— Setting Your Thoughts Spinning ———

How do we use verbs to tell our readers that something has already happened? What about telling readers something that will happen later?

——————— Pulling It All Together ———————

The **past** tense is used to tell the reader that something has already happened. The action is over and done with. For example:

> Willis **drove** Jackie to the clinic.

> The police siren **faded** into the distance.

Can you see that each of these actions is no longer taking place?

Most past tense verbs end in *d* or *ed*. Many, however, are what we call **irregular**. These verbs change form in other ways. For example, the past tense of *drive* is not *drived*, but *drove*. The past tense of *go* is not *goed*, but *went*. We will not cover these forms in this writing book. You can find lists of irregular verb forms in any English grammar book. You can also find out whether a verb has an irregular past tense form by looking in a dictionary. Look up the word under the present tense (for example, *go*.) If the verb is irregular, the forms will be listed right after the pronunciation. If the past tense is formed simply by adding *d* or *ed*, no forms are listed. The past tense form of irregular verbs are important to know.

The **future** verb tense is for actions that will begin and end later. The future tense form is made by adding *will* or *shall* to the verbs. For example:

> Jessie **will walk** to work on Friday.

> The Cubs **shall win** the pennant next year.

Do you see that the verbs in these sentences show that these actions have not taken place yet? They will happen in the future.

——————————— Working Out ———————————

Part A

Rick, a story writer, is always taking notes in his notebook. Last week he took notes to use in his new story. However, Rick needs all his sentences to be written in the past tense instead of the present.

Rewrite Rick's notes for his new story. Change every <u>present</u> tense to the <u>past</u> tense.

> The rocky hill overlooks the riverfront. The meeting is scheduled for midnight. It is lonely up on that hill. Looking down at the riverfront, Jake Blaine notices two headlights. They are making their way among the maze of warehouses and piers to the foot of the hill. The headlights are cut off. Jake hears car doors slam. Two men begin to climb the hill.

Part B

Rick wants to write a letter to a friend to predict great success for his story. Finish the letter for him using the **future tense** as much as you can. Write at least five sentences.

Dear Ralph,

My story will be great.

_____

_____

_____

_____

_____

_____

Sincerely,

Rick

SAMPLE ANSWERS ARE ON PAGE 166.

——————— On Your Own ———————

Many people keep diaries or journals. A journal is something like a writer's notebook with dated entries. You write in it once a day or once a week. You may want to summarize your day. You may just want to write down what is important to you.

Sometimes people keep track of their personal goals in their journals. Sometimes they even keep financial records. Mostly, however, we use journals to talk to ourselves. We write about the things we need to think through.

Write down the following headings and leave room to write next to each. Now fill in the information for yesterday or today.

Date:

Goals to meet today:

Writing done:

Personal thoughts:

If you think a journal would be useful to you, use a notebook. Set up your pages like you did above and try to write in your journal every day.

Using Time Words in Sentences

—— Setting Your Thoughts Spinning ——

How many ways to show time in sentences do you already know? You learned about using "when" words to describe action in Chapter 1. You have also just learned how verbs show time. Are there other words that help the writer tell the reader when something happened?

—————— Pulling It All Together ——————

Put the following events in the order in which they happened. Put a <u>1</u> next to what happened first, a <u>2</u> next to what happened second, etc.

_____ Grace prepared the meal.

_____ She bought plenty of groceries.

_____ She needed money for the groceries, so she went to the bank.

_____ Grace decided to have company for dinner.

_____ The guests arrived and sat down to eat.

How can you best describe to your reader the order in which these things happened? Using time words like those in the chart below will help. On a separate sheet of paper, write a short paragraph using the sentences above and some of the time words from the chart.

first	second	third	afterward
next	later	finally	then
soon	last	meanwhile	

Here are some examples of sentences using time words.

Next, Grace prepared the meal.

Finally, the guests arrived and sat down to eat.

Notice that, when a time word comes at the beginning of a sentence, you should put a comma after it.

Working Out

Part A

Fill in the blanks with appropriate time words from the chart on page 36. Try to use a variety of words.

The process for writing a business letter is very simple.

_____, you must find clean stationery and a good pen.

_____, put the date and your home address at the top

right-hand corner of the paper. _____, skip a couple of

lines and, at the left margin, write the name and address of the

person you are writing. Begin your letter a couple of lines underneath

with "Dear So and So." _____, skip another couple of

lines and begin the body of the letter. _____, close your

letter with a phrase such as "Sincerely yours." _____,

sign your name and print it underneath.

Part B

Jot down in your notebook or on a piece of paper everything you do at <u>ONE</u> of the following events. Put these actions in the order in which they happen. Next, use lots of time words and "when" words to write a paragraph about the event.

1. baseball game
2. wedding
3. church service
4. picnic

_____

_____

_____

_____

_____

_____

_____

_____

_____

_____

_____

SAMPLE ANSWERS ARE ON PAGE 166.

Closing the Chapter

————————— You Have Learned —————————

1. how verbs can show time in a sentence.

2. to write sentences in the present, past, and future tenses.

3. how to set up a journal.

4. different time words and phrases you can use in your sentences.

————— Another Chance to Work with Tenses —————

Write a letter to a friend or relative. The letter should have three parts or paragraphs. Use time words whenever possible.

First, write about how you and your family are doing. Mention your job, health, or current activities. Use the present tense for this part of the letter.

Second, write about something that happened recently—such as the last vacation you had or a job you once held. In this part you share memories with your friend or relative. Use the past tense here.

Third, write about something you have to look forward to, such as an upcoming party or an activity you will take part in over the weekend. Use the future tense here.

Chapter 4

Watching Your Words

———— Your Chapter Goals Are ————

1. to get ideas for choosing interesting, colorful words.
2. to learn which words to use with care.
3. to get rid of repeated ideas in your sentences.

Have you ever stumbled around trying to find the right word to use in a sentence? This chapter will help you choose the right word. You will also learn when some words should not be used.

Finding the Right Word

─── Setting Your Thoughts Spinning ───

Have you ever heard of games like Rumor and Pass It On? These are games in which a group of people make up a story by putting their ideas together.

For instance, in Pass It On, a person makes up the first line of a story. The next person says the first thing that comes into his head and adds this idea to the story. The other people in the group add to these ideas to complete the story.

We do something interesting in games like Pass It On. We say the first thing that comes to our mind when we hear something else. A person could hear "auto mechanic" and then think "good pay." Another person might hear the same thing and say "Mike's Garage."

In this lesson, you'll learn how you can get started writing by jotting down what first comes to mind. This **brainstorming** activity is similar to the activity you did on page 15, Putting More Action in Your Sentences.

─── Pulling It All Together ───

Think of words as ideas and use words to think of more words. Take some time to write down whatever comes to mind to get your ideas together before you write.

For instance, suppose you want to describe your new house to a friend. Write down the things you want to describe. For example:

> backyard
>
> garage
>
> windows
>
> living room

Now think about these words one at a time. Try to think of words and phrases that will help you describe each topic. Here are some words one person matched with this list.

> **backyard**—tiny but pretty
>
> **garage**—two-car
>
> **windows**—lots
>
> **living room**—very comfortable

Sentences are now easier to write for each topic.

1. The house has a tiny but pretty backyard.
2. In the back of the house is a two-car garage.
3. There are lots of windows everywhere.
4. The living room is very comfortable.

You can also link actions with nouns. For example, think about these words: *secretary*, *foreman*, *audience*, *guns*. Here are the actions that one person linked up with these words.

secretary—types

foreman—shouted

audience—booed

guns—protect

Use the lines below to write some sentences using these pairs.

_____

_____

_____

_____

Working Out

Part A

Help yourself start writing. Look at the following list of topics. Write down the first thing that comes to mind to help you describe these topics.

bride   _____

groom   _____

ceremony   _____

weather   _____

reception   _____

mother of the bride   _____

mother of the groom   _____

laughter   _____

tears   _____

Part B

Use the words and phrases you came up with in Part A to describe a wedding. Feel free to add any other ideas you'd like. You don't have to use all the phrases from Part A. Try to write seven to ten sentences.

A SAMPLE PARAGRAPH IS ON PAGE 167.

Slang Words/Stale Words

———— Setting Your Thoughts Spinning ————

What goes through your mind when you hear these phrases? *Twenty-three skidoo. That's boss! Far out! Totally, man. See ya later, alligator!*

Do you have fond memories of these words, or do they seem a bit outdated?

———————— Pulling It All Together ————————

The expressions above are examples of slang. **Slang**, a kind of informal language, is different from one generation to the next. *Twenty-three skidoo* was slang in the 1920s. *See ya later, alligator* was used in the 1950s. *Far out* is from the 1960s and *totally* belongs to the 1970s.

Be careful of using slang in your writing. Think about your audience. Sometimes slang can be a common language for you to share with someone else. However, it can often set you apart from people who don't speak the same language. For example, you would not want to use slang in a memo to your boss.

Jargon also sets people apart from one another. Jargon is used by people in certain jobs. Each job has its own jargon. If you are a clerk typist, you may call a *typographical error* a *typo*. Jargon can also be a word only experts would know. For instance, a scientist may use the word *arachnid* instead of *spider*. Be careful when using jargon away from your job or fellow experts.

Clichés are expressions we hear over and over again. *He wears many hats* is a cliché meaning *He has many different responsibilities. When hell freezes over* is a cliché that means *never*. Usually you should avoid using too many clichés when you write. Try to use original ideas.

——— Working Out ———

Cross out any slang, jargon, or clichés in these sentences. Rewrite each sentence using your own words. The first one is done for you.

1. I'm already hip to that.

   I already know that.

2. Trisha's New Year's Eve party was a total wipeout.

3. Well, that's six of one—a half dozen of the other.

4. You can take that to the bank!

5. Tom is so crabby that we're all walking on eggshells around here.

6. Her new dress is totally out of control.

7. I didn't want us to get into a heavy rap.

8. Give it to me straight and don't pull any punches.

SAMPLE ANSWERS ARE ON PAGE 167.

——— On Your Own ———

List **FIVE** more clichés or slang words you have heard people use. Start your own dictionary of expressions you should be careful using. Then list some different ways you could say the same things expressed in these clichés and slang phrases.

Getting Carried Away

———— Setting Your Thoughts Spinning ————

Do you ever get carried away when you're talking? Have you ever noticed that you're repeating yourself? Do you do this when you're excited, angry, concentrating, or tired?

Try to think of when you might repeat yourself. Remember, emotions can change our writing too. We may write things we don't mean or write them over and over again in the same letter or paragraph—just to make a point.

———————— Pulling It All Together ————————

Not all repetition is bad. Sometimes it is good to repeat what was said before. It reminds the reader of something important. Repetition also helps convince someone that something is important. For example, in a famous speech, President Lincoln used the expression, "of the people, by the people, and for the people. . ." He used this repetition on purpose to emphasize the importance of people to the government.

The trick is to be in control of your words. Repeat when you want to repeat something. However, be careful and reread what you have written. You may have been unaware that you were repeating yourself.

Look for words and phrases that say basically the same thing. Chances are that you can take some of these ideas out. Where is the repeated idea in this sentence?

I think this car needs a tune-up, in my opinion.

Can you see that *I think* and *in my opinion* mean the same thing? There is no need to use both of these expressions in one sentence. Try to find the repetition in the following sentence.

Rupert's neighborhood where he lives is pretty and beautiful.

First of all, *neighborhood* means the same thing as *where he lives*, so take one of these expressions out. Second, *pretty* and *beautiful* also mean the same thing. Only one of these adjectives is necessary. Rewrite the sentence this way:

Rupert's neighborhood is beautiful.

Working Out

The Atlas Record of the Month Club keeps sending you records. You have already canceled your subscription twice. Now the club is sending you bills. You write the following letter in anger, and then you realize that it has a lot of repeated ideas in it. Cross out all unnecessary repetition and rewrite the letter. When you are done, reread your letter to see how much smoother it sounds.

> To whom it may concern:
>
> I am writing to you to communicate with you about the enclosed bills inside.
>
> In October and November, I sent letters in the mail informing you that I am telling you that I want to cancel and stop my subscription to the Atlas Record of the Month Club. As of this date today, I am still receiving records. I have been sending and mailing back these records for two months.
>
> I should not be billed or charged for records sent to me after I canceled and stopped my subscription. I should bill you for the stamps and postage it took to return and send back the records each month.
>
> Please stop, halt, and end all shipments of records and stop, halt, and end all billing and charging.
>
> Thank you!

_____
_____
_____
_____
_____
_____
_____
_____
_____
_____
_____

THE IMPROVED LETTER IS ON PAGE 167.

On Your Own

You work for the Customer Service Department at Atlas Record of the Month Club. Write an answer to the letter above. Apologize to the customer for any inconvenience and explain the problem. Make sure you repeat ideas only when necessary.

Closing the Chapter

——————— You Have Learned ———————

1. some ways to find the right word to use.

2. some words and expressions you should be careful about using.

3. to watch out for unnecessary repetition in your writing.

——————— Working On Your Writing ———————

You have won a new convertible or $15,000 in a raffle. Now you have been asked to help publicize that raffle. You are to write at least ten lines about how you feel about having won. Talk about your plans for the car or money as well. Watch out for repetition, slang or jargon, and clichés.

Section II

Framing

Chapter 5

Adding Information to Sentences

──────── **Your Chapter Goals Are** ────────

1. to begin to use a greater variety of sentences.

2. to add to the amount of information in your sentences.

3. to learn how to combine ideas from different sentences.

We do not have to write all our sentences the same way. Nor do we have to write a separate sentence for each fact our readers should know. A single sentence can contain a good deal of information.

In this chapter, you will learn how to combine facts from shorter sentences into longer, more informative sentences.

Connecting Subjects

—— Setting Your Thoughts Spinning ——

Have you ever said something like this?

"Jack will be leaving soon. Oh, Mary will be leaving
soon too."

Did you really need two sentences to tell someone about Jack and Mary? If you had remembered about Mary, you could have said:

"Jack and Mary will be leaving soon."

When we talk, we cannot rework our sentences. When we write, we can.

—— Pulling It All Together ——

Both Jack and Mary were leaving. Because they were both doing the same thing, we could put them in the same sentence. We use the connecting word *and* to do this. Here's another example:

Paul went bowling.
+ **Anita** went bowling.

= **Paul and Anita** went bowling.

Sometimes you will need to change some words in your sentences when combining with *and*. These words will have to be changed from singular (meaning one) to plural (meaning more than one). The most important word you may have to change from singular to plural is your verb. For example:

My mother **is** a crossing guard.
+ My sister **is** a crossing guard too.

= My mother and sister **are** crossing guard**s**.

Notice we had to use *are* instead of *is*. You also needed to make *crossing guard* plural by adding an *s*.

> You must change verbs from singular (one) to plural (more than one) when using *and*. You may have to change other words to plural forms as well.

Now combine the following sentences using *and*. Notice how one cue card tells you what verb to substitute. Another cue card tells you that *salesman* must be put in its plural form.

Joshua was a shoe salesman. were
+ Manny was a shoe salesman. salesmen

= _____

Remember that some verb forms are used with plural subjects and some are not. Chapter 11 will give you more information on which verb form is correct to use.

Practice combining subjects with the sentences below. Make sure you change singular words to plural when necessary. The cue cards provided will give you a clue.

My husband wanted to throw a big party.

I wanted to throw a big party.

_____

_____

Our daughter was in charge of decorations.   were

Our son was in charge of decorations.

_____

_____

Pat was a bartender.   were

Carlos was a bartender.   bartenders

_____

_____

By 7:00 our house was full of people.   were

Our yard was full of people.

_____

_____

——— Working Out ———

Rewrite the letter below. Look for short sentences you can combine by joining the subjects with *and*. Remember to replace singular words with plural words when necessary.

Dear Cathy,

The party was great. Dean was there. His wife Virginia was there too. It was good to see them. Lauren was a guest. Betty was also a guest. They asked how you were.

Our new chair looks just great. Our desk also looks great. Mark is enjoying the new place. I am enjoying it too. You should come and see it. Mom should come too.

SAMPLE ANSWERS ARE ON PAGE 168.

Connecting Other Nouns

———— Setting Your Thoughts Spinning ————

If we can combine subjects, can we combine other nouns too? How can these two sentences be combined into one?

> Rhonda gave Marcie a new coat.
> + She gave Marcie a hat too.
>
> = _____

———————— Pulling It All Together ————————

The first two sentences above can be combined into:

> Rhonda gave Marcie a new coat and hat.

Since both the coat and hat were given to Marcie by the same person, these words can be joined by *and* in the same sentence.

> You can use *and* to join nouns following the same subject
> and verb.

The words same subject include a case such as this:

> Harry is a welder.
> + He is an electrician too.
>
> = Harry is a welder and an electrician.

We knew that *he* meant *Harry*. Therefore, the subjects were the same.

There is another place to look for nouns to combine. This is after words such as *on*, *to*, *by*, *for*, and others.

> The tickets will be sold on Friday.
> + The tickets will be sold on Saturday.
>
> = The tickets will be sold on Friday and Saturday.

———————————— Working Out ————————————

This exercise will allow you to practice combining nouns in your sentences. First fill in the blanks with your own ideas. Then combine the nouns in each pair of sentences. Remember to change the verbs and other nouns to plural, if necessary. The first one is done for you.

1. Yesterday I went to *a ball game*.

   I also went to *a party* yesterday.

   Yesterday I went to a ball game and a party.

2. A person I really admire is _____.

Another person I really admire is _____.

_____

3. For dinner today, I had _____.

I also had _____ for dinner today.

_____

4. One of my least favorite activities is _____.

Another one of my least favorite activities is _____.

_____

5. I hate a song that is sung by _____.

The song is also sung by _____.

_____

6. My closest friend is a _____.

He (or she) is also a _____.

_____

SAMPLE ANSWERS ARE ON PAGES 168-69.

────────────────── **On Your Own** ──────────────────

Here is a short memo to the clerical staff in an office. Rewrite this memo. Look for short sentences you can combine by

    1. joining nouns after the same subject and verb.

    2. joining nouns after the same connecting word.

To: The Clerical Staff

From: Clerical Supervisor

Beginning Monday, May 16, some of you will get new lunch hours. Some of you will get new job assignments. We need clerk typists to work on the yearly financial report. We need file clerks to work on it too. Mr. Paterno and I will be meeting about these assignments on Thursday. We will be meeting on Friday as well.

We will post the new lunch hours on the bulletin board the following Monday. We will post the new job assignments as well.

Making Lists

—— Setting Your Thoughts Spinning ——

We make lists all the time. We make grocery lists and lists of things to do. We make lists of things to pack for a trip. But how do we make lists in sentences?

—————— Pulling It All Together ——————

Lists contain three or more items. The items are separated by commas. We can make lists by using the connecting word *and*. A list of words combined by using *and* and commas is called a **series**. We use *and* the same way we connected pairs of words in the last lesson. For example:

> **The milkman** gets paid on Friday.
> + **The paperboy** gets paid on Friday.
> + **The baby-sitter** gets paid on Friday.
>
> = **The milkman, the paperboy, and the baby-sitter**
>   get paid on Friday.

Remember, when combining subjects with *and*, be on the lookout for singular words that need to be changed to plurals. Especially watch for the verbs. For example, the verb *gets* in the first three sentences above had to be changed to the plural, *get*. This is because you would say, "They *get* paid," not "They *gets* paid."

Just as you learned with pairs of nouns in the last lesson, lists of other nouns can also be combined using *and*. For example:

> **1.**   The Elk Lodge serves **roast beef** on Tuesdays.
> + The Elk Lodge serves **potatoes** on Tuesdays.
> + The Elk Lodge serves **broccoli** too.
>
> = The Elk Lodge serves **roast beef, potatoes, and broccoli** on Tuesdays.

> **2.**   Jack took Beth to **the Jazz Club**.
> + Jack took Beth to **Pearl's Cafe**.
> + He also took Beth to **Klinger Park**.
>
> = Jack took Beth to the **Jazz Club, Pearl's Cafe, and Klinger Park**.

Making lists in sentences sometimes causes problems for writers. Here are two important things to watch out for. 1) If your list has less than three nouns in it, it is not really a series. Therefore, do not use a comma.

Wrong: Freddie brought us a flower, and a card.
         (only two items)

Right: Freddie brought us a flower and a card.
         (no comma)

Right: Freddie brought us candy, a flower, and a card.
         (three items and a comma)

2) After you write down your list of nouns in a sentence, go back and look again. Each item between the commas should be a noun.

Wrong: My mom should go to the beach, the park, and
                                  noun   *noun*

         go to the department stores on her day off.
         verb

Right: My mom should go to the beach, the park, and
                                  noun   *noun*

         the department stores on her day off.
           noun

⎯⎯⎯⎯⎯ Working Out ⎯⎯⎯⎯⎯

Combine these sentences. Remember to include commas where necessary. The first one is done for you.

BECOMING A CITIZEN

1. To become a citizen someone must be at least eighteen years old.

   Someone must be at least a permanent resident.

   Someone must be at least a moral person.

   To become a citizen someone must be at least eighteen years old, a permanent resident, and a moral person.

2. To apply for citizenship, a person must turn in a petition.

   A person must turn in a fingerprint card.

   A person must turn in three photographs of himself.

   _____

   _____

3. Husbands must apply separately.

   Wives must apply separately.

   Children must apply separately.

   _____

   _____

4. There are two witnesses at a citizenship test.
There is an applicant at a citizenship test.
There is an examiner at a citizenship test.

_____

_____

5. At the final hearing there is a judge.
At the final hearing there is an applicant.
At the final hearing there is an examiner.

_____

_____

6. Applicants for citizenship have to make it through a petition.
They have to make it through a test.
They have to make it through a final hearing.
They have to make it through a loyalty oath.

_____

_____

7. My grandparents are naturalized citizens.
My aunt is a naturalized citizen.
My uncle is a naturalized citizen.

_____

_____

8. My brother saw each of them declared citizens.
My sister saw each of them declared citizens.
I saw each of them declared citizens.

_____

_____

ANSWERS ARE ON PAGE 169.

On Your Own

Part A

Think about the lists you might make from day to day. Complete these sentences with lists of three or four people, places, or things. Remember to separate items in your lists with commas.

1. Today I need to get in touch with _____

_____.

2. _____ will probably

stop by sometime today.

3. I need _____ from

the grocery store.

4. I should go to _____

_____.

5. For lunch I had _____

_____.

Part B

The following paragraph has four errors. Look for lists of words combined with commas and *and*. Remember that each of these words must be a noun. Also remember that the list must have at least three nouns, or a comma is not needed.

Underline the four errors you find and rewrite the sentences correctly.

Jack's room was more like the family room than a bedroom. He had a great stereo, a television set, and had a video recorder. His family, and friends spent more time in there than anywhere in the house. People would bring tapes, records, and sometimes would arrive with favorite books to discuss. Jack's room was really the center, and heart of all activity.

Connecting Actions

—————— Setting Your Thoughts Spinning ——————

Imagine these actions taking place:

> The quarterback dropped back.
>
> He looked around.
>
> He threw the ball.

Do we have to write a separate sentence for each action? Can we put more than one action into a sentence?

————————— Pulling It All Together —————————

You have already used *and* to make lists and combine names. You can also use *and* to connect actions.

> You can use *and* to combine actions when the same subject is performing the actions.

The sentences about the quarterback could be combined. You can combine them by making a list of the quarterback's actions.

> The quarterback dropped back, looked around, and threw the ball.

Remember, when making lists you must use commas to separate the items. Also make sure you are separating actions, not subjects and actions.

Actions, like names, can also be combined two at a time. For example:

> Walter washed the dishes.
> + Walter also dried the dishes.
> = Walter washed and dried the dishes.

Connecting actions can add variety to your sentences. Listing actions in order (as with the quarterback) can also help your reader picture when the actions took place.

————————————— Working Out —————————————

This exercise provides practice in combining actions in sentences. The following sentences need to be rewritten on the lines below. Rewrite them by combining pairs of actions or by making lists of actions. The brackets and cue cards will tell you which sentences to combine. The first one is done for you.

⎧Danny always passed better than any other kid.
⎨He always ran better than any other kid.
⎩He always kicked better than any other kid.

{ Now he plays quarterback at the local high school. `and`
{ He runs track at the local high school too.

{ I still coach him. `and`
{ I still encourage him.

{ I remember one game in particular. `and`
{ I still tell people about one game in particular.

{ Danny hustled his heart out. `and` `,,`
{ He passed his heart out.
{ He ran his heart out too.

{ He is working on becoming an All-American someday. `and`
{ He is planning on becoming an All-American someday.

{ I scrimp to send him to college. `and`
{ I save to send him to college.

Danny always passed, ran, and kicked better than any other kid.

_____

_____

_____

_____

A SAMPLE PARAGRAPH IS ON PAGE 169.

───────────── **On Your Own** ─────────────

Complete these sentences by listing two or more actions. Remember to use commas when necessary.

1. When I get up in the morning I _____

_____

2. Before I go to bed I _____

_____

3. Everyday at work I _____

_____

4. Someday I will _____

_____

Combining When, Where, and How

———— Setting Your Thoughts Spinning ————

Can any of these sentences be combined?

what   1.   A semitrailer truck jackknifed.

how   2.   It jackknifed at a weird angle.

where   3.   It jackknifed on the expressway.

when   4.   It jackknifed during the morning rush hour.

Do you see that the one sentence below contains all of this information? It tells you what, when, where, and how.

A semitrailer truck jackknifed at a weird angle on the expressway during the morning rush hour.

———— Pulling It All Together ————

You can combine phrases that tell when, where, and how. Again, look at your subjects and verbs for clues as to when to combine. Your subjects and verbs will tell you if the same thing is being talked about from sentence to sentence.

1.   Raoul wanted Sherry to meet him.
+ He wanted Sherry to meet him at the park.   `where`
+ He wanted Sherry to meet him after closing.   `when`

= Raoul wanted Sherry to meet him **at the park after closing.**

2.   The flowers were arranged in the old vase.   `where`
+ The flowers were arranged with loving care.   `how`

= The flowers were arranged **with loving care in the old vase.**

Remember to watch the sentences you read and write for words that tell where, when, or how. See if these ideas can be combined with others in one sentence.

Working Out

Part A

This exercise allows you to practice combining sentences and facts about when, where, and how. Combine each set, watching the cue cards to see what facts to combine.

For instance, the cue cards *when* and *where* tell you to use words showing when and where to combine the sentences. The first one is done for you.

CAREFUL CONSUMERS

1. Marcia throws out leftovers.

   She throws them out after two days.   when

   Marcia throws out leftovers after two days.

2. Mr. Sanchez always reads labels.

   He reads labels on cans.   where

   He reads labels at the grocery store.   where

   _____

   _____

3. People should watch their fat intake.

   They should watch it carefully.   how

   They should watch it when dieting.   when

   _____

   _____

4. Ed Lavin always buys a new car.

   He buys it from a well-known dealership.   where

   He always buys it during midseason sales.   when

   _____

   _____

5. Julie likes to compare prices.

   She compares prices at various stores.   where

   She compares prices before buying anything.   when

   _____

   _____

6. Mrs. Bing has a life insurance policy.

She has it in a safe deposit box.   where

She has it at the bank.   where

_____

_____

Part B

Practice adding more information to sentences. Answer the questions after each of the following sentences. Then combine the information in one sentence. The first one is done for you.

1. The dog bit a stranger.

WHEN? *yesterday*

WHERE? *on the leg*

HOW? *suddenly*

Yesterday the dog suddenly bit a stranger on the leg.

2. The income tax forms sat.

WHERE? _____

WHEN?   _____

HOW?   _____

_____

3. She looked at the tray of desserts.

WHERE? _____

WHEN?   _____

HOW?   _____

_____

4. The thief left the apartment.

WHERE? _____

WHEN?   _____

HOW?   _____

_____

5. He answered the question.

WHERE? _____

WHEN? _____

HOW? _____

_____

6. The window opened.

WHERE? _____

WHEN? _____

HOW? _____

_____

SAMPLE ANSWERS ARE ON PAGES 169-70.

———————— **Trick of the Trade** ————————

Up to now you have been putting "when," "where," and "how" words toward the end of sentences. Now try shifting these words around. It creates even more variety in your sentences.

For instance, some words showing when, where, or how can be moved to the beginning of sentences. Instead of saying:

> Julie likes to compare prices at various stores before buying anything.

You can say:

> Before buying anything, Julie likes to compare prices at various stores.

Notice how a comma is used when these words introduce the main part of the sentence.

Practice shifting groups of words to the front of your sentences. Remember to use a comma before beginning the main part of the sentence. Take each sentence you wrote in Part B above and move one or two of the "when," "where," and "how" words to the front of the sentence.

Drawing Pictures for People

─── Setting Your Thoughts Spinning ───

In this lesson, you'll have a chance to write about this picture. On a separate piece of paper, write down all of the ideas you think of when you look at this scene. You'll probably think of lots of describing words. Let your imagination go and write down everything. Don't go to Working Out until you have a list of 10 ideas or more.

────────── Working Out ──────────

Part A

Now put your ideas into sentences. Try to describe the scene to someone who cannot look at it as you can. Give your reader as clear a picture as possible.

   Try to put ideas together in your sentences. Look through your ideas to see if there are any that could be combined somehow. Use the combining techniques you've learned so far in this book. You can put describing words together in a series just as you did with nouns and actions. For example:

      The street was empty.
   + The street was dark.
   + The street was silent.

   = The street was empty, dark, and silent.

Part B

The writer of the story on the next page wanted to describe the picture. In doing so, however, this writer used too many short, choppy sentences. Rewrite this story on the lines given. In this exercise, you will use all the skills learned in this chapter. Combine sentences whenever possible by

   1. joining subjects.

   2. joining other nouns.

   3. connecting actions.

   4. making a series.

   5. joining describing words.

   6. putting groups of words showing when, where, or how into the same sentence.

A HIDDEN TREASURE

I was stacking old magazines. I was stacking them in my uncle's basement. Suddenly I noticed something strange. It was a huge captain's trunk. I pushed. I pulled. I finally turned the trunk around. Inside was an Indian blanket. Inside there was some pottery. Inside there was a long rolled-up paper.

I spread the paper. I spread it on the floor. It was a drawing of an old Indian couple. It was a drawing of the couple on a wooden porch. Their faces stared back at me. The man's face was lined. It was wrinkled. He was frowning. He was staring straight ahead. The woman's face was softer. It was less wrinkled. It was more cheerful.

They wore work clothes. The man's overalls were baggy. They were too long for him. He wore a belt. He wore a work shirt. He wore a bandana too. He had a cowboy hat. He had it on his head. He held a tobacco pouch. He held it in his hand. The woman wore a long dress. She wore an apron. The wind had blown the apron. She was holding it with her hands. She was holding it down. The woman's dress was hooked with safety pins. She wore a cap. She wore earrings. She wore laced boots.

There was a screen door behind the couple. There was a window. There were two signs too. They must have been standing in front of a store or trading post.

Who could have drawn this picture? It was a mystery. I took it home. I framed it. I sold it to an art gallery.

I was stacking old magazines in my uncle's basement.

_____

_____

_____

_____

_____

_____

DISCUSSION OF PART A AND A SAMPLE STORY IS ON PAGE 170.

───────── Trick of the Trade ─────────

Writers should try to compare their work to other writing. Compare your story above to the original one. How did you improve it? Does yours have have more sentence variety? Does yours sound smoother? Now look at the rewritten story in the answer sampler. Could you have improved yours more? Could you have used a greater variety of sentences?

Closing the Chapter

——— You Have Learned That ———

1. a variety of sentences can be made by connecting words or making a series.

2. you can combine sentences by joining nouns, actions, and describing words.

3. you can add to sentences by telling where, when, and how.

——— Review Exercise ———

Combine the sets of sentences below on a separate piece of paper. Put your new sentences in paragraph form.

1. Writing memos can be difficult.
   Writing business letters can be difficult.

2. A clerk needs to write on the job.
   A secretary needs to write on the job.
   A manager needs to write on the job.

3. You have to watch your spelling.
   You have to watch your punctuation.
   You have to watch your grammar.

4. Good writers carefully organize their letters.
   They carefully write their letters.
   They carefully revise their letters.

5. Poorly written memos can be confusing.
   They can be confusing when time is short.
   They can be confusing in meetings.

6. We all should consider our audience.
   We should consider them well.
   We should consider them before writing memos.

Chapter 6

Combining Sentences to Describe

──────── **Your Chapter Goals Are** ────────

1. to learn how to connect whole sentences.

2. to learn more about putting sentences inside other sentences.

3. to learn more about describing people, things, and actions for your reader.

In this chapter you will be making more long sentences out of shorter ones. You will do this by combining the ideas in the shorter sentences in certain ways. Most of the time, you will relate these ideas by using connecting words such as *but, and, who, however*, and others.

Being Similar

——— Setting Your Thoughts Spinning ———

Sometimes we talk about how similar things or people are. Have you ever talked about how much alike two people from the same family are or how much alike two cities or neighborhoods are?

What are some of the words that help us recognize when things are similar?

——— Pulling It All Together ———

You have already learned to use *and* to join similar words from different sentences. For example:

      My mother is a crossing guard.
 +   My sister is a crossing guard.

 =   My mother and my sister are crossing guards.

You could have used **both . . . and** to show how the ideas in each sentence were similar. For example:

Both my mother **and** sister are crossing guards.

Both . . . and emphasizes the fact that there is something similar about the mother and sister. Now let's look at another way of showing how ideas can be combined to show similarity.

> The word *and* used with a comma can be used to join two complete sentences.

By using the word *and* to join sentences, you are showing that the ideas are similar or related in some way.

      Bill will wash the dishes after supper.
 +   I will dry them.

 =   Bill will wash the dishes after supper, **and** I will dry them.

Working Out

This exercise has two purposes. One purpose is for you to practice combining sentences with *and* plus a comma. The second purpose is for you to practice comparing things. Because of the second reason, you will also use *both . . . and* to join some of these sentences.

Combine each pair of sentences using the cue cards on the right. The first one is done for you.

TWO JOBS

1. Joe Smalley needs an extra job.   `both` `and`

Pat Silver needs an extra job.   `need`

Both Joe Smalley and Pat Silver need an extra job.

2. There are openings busing dishes.

Jobs pumping gas aren't hard to find.   `and` `,`

_____

_____

3. There are eleven restaurants in town.

Three service stations are open all night.   `and` `,`

_____

_____

4. Busing dishes requires little experience.   `both` `and`

Pumping gas requires little experience.   `require`

_____

_____

5. The restaurant job requires only filling out an application.

The gas station job requires only a short interview.   `and` `,`

_____

_____

6. The restaurant job has suitable hours.   `both` `and`

The gas station job has suitable hours.   `have`

_____

_____

ANSWERS ARE ON PAGE 171.

Being Different

—— Setting Your Thoughts Spinning ——

We talk about how people, actions, or things are different. How would you connect sentences to show differences? For example:

> Volkswagens are made in Germany.
> + Toyotas are made in Japan.
>
> = Volkswagens are made in Germany, **but** Toyotas are made in Japan.

Is *but* the only word you could use to show differences?

—————— Pulling It All Together ——————

> You can use a comma and *but* or a comma and *yet* to combine two sentences. You do this when you want to show the difference between two things.

You can contrast people's actions. For example:

> She liked the dress.
> + She didn't buy it.
>
> = She liked the dress, **yet** she didn't buy it.

You can also contrast things, people, or places. For example:

> A soap opera may last for years.
> + A situation comedy may last only a season.
>
> = A soap opera may last for years, **yet** a situation comedy may last only a season.

To show contrast, you can also combine sentences with *however*. When joining two sentences, *however* must have a semicolon (;) before it and a comma (,) after it.

> 1.   Vernon said he wasn't sick.
>   + He looked rather pale to me.
>
>   = Vernon said he wasn't sick; **however,** he looked rather pale to me.
>
> 2.   The sedan is a roomier car.
>   + The compact gets better gas mileage.
>
>   = The sedan is a roomier car; **however,** the compact gets better gas mileage.

Notice how in all these examples two complete sentences are put together. There is a subject and verb on each side of the connecting word. That is why some form of punctuation is needed with the connecting word.

Working Out

This exercise has two purposes. One purpose is for you to practice combining sentences with *but*, *yet*, or *however*. The second purpose is for you to practice contrasting facts or ideas in sentences. Combine each pair of sentences using the cue cards provided. The first one is done for you.

TOO SOON FOR THE GOOD OLD DAYS

1. I consider myself very young.

My children think I'm old-fashioned. `yet` `,`

I consider myself very young, yet my children think I'm old-fashioned.

2. Things were different back when I was young. `;` `however`

I still think we were ahead of our time. `,`

_____

_____

3. Our generation had certain commitments.

This generation seems to have different ones. `,` `but`

_____

_____

4. We made progress with civil rights.

People now seem concerned about other things. `,` `but`

_____

_____

5. Many of us are veterans of Viet Nam. `;` `however`

Many of us fought against that war. `,`

_____

_____

6. In the sixties, social action was important.

Today people seem to think only of themselves. `,` `yet`

_____

_____

7. Hippies gave away flowers.

Today punk rockers wear razor blades and spikes.   [,] [but]

_____

_____

8. In our day, songs had messages.

Today's songs are too commercial.   [,] [but]

_____

_____

9. We wanted people to be positive.   [;] [however]

People became more negative over the years.   [,]

_____

_____

10. I don't want to live in the past.

I sure do miss the 1960s.   [,] [but]

_____

_____

ANSWERS ARE ON PAGE 171.

On Your Own

Do you agree with "Too Soon for the Good Old Days"? Maybe you would like to contrast your opinions with the writer's.

Complete the following sentences using *but*, *yet*, or *however* and your own opinions. The first one is done for you. Remember the comma and semicolon when they are needed!

1. The writer misses the 1960s *, but perhaps she is remembering only the best parts of that time.*

2. Things were different in the 1960s _____

3. Today people just think of themselves _____

4. Some songs in the 1960s had messages _____

5. People have become more negative _____

6. The writer doesn't want to live in the past _____

Naming Names

———— Setting Your Thoughts Spinning ————

How much information should you give your reader? Which of the sentences below would be the most helpful to someone?

Jack Riley will handle your complaint.

Jack Riley, a building inspector, will handle your complaint.

Jack Riley, an experienced building inspector, will handle your complaint.

The first sentence leaves you asking, "Who is Jack Riley?" The second sentence might leave you asking, "Is he experienced?" The third sentence makes you feel more secure.

———— Pulling It All Together ————

Notice how *building inspector* is another name for Jack Riley. It told us who Jack was. Words that are used as other names for people, places, or things are called appositives. An **appositive** renames the noun it follows in order to give more information.

Appositives can help us combine sentences. For example:

Fred constantly talks about his job.

Fred is my brother-in-law.

To make this writing less repetitious and more interesting, these sentences could be combined into one.

Fred, **my brother-in-law**, constantly talks about his job.

> When you use an appositive, you must use a comma before it and after it (unless it is at the end of a sentence).

Appositives can be used to identify anyone or anything—not just the subject of the sentence. For example:

We had a picnic out at Stokely.

Stokely is an old mansion.

We had a picnic out at Stokely, **an old mansion**.

Notice that, when the appositive is at the end of the sentence, you simply put a comma before it and a period after it.

Working Out

Practice combining short sentences by using commas where necessary. The first one is done for you.

INTERMINGLE

1. There was an article in today's paper about Intermingle.
   Intermingle is a dating service.

   There was an article in today's paper about Intermingle, a dating service.

2. Barry Friedman wrote the story.
   Barry is an insurance salesman.

   _____

   _____

3. Barry and his wife met through Intermingle.
   His wife is a hairstylist.

   _____

   _____

4. Intermingle videotapes its clients.
   Intermingle is a modern service.

   _____

   _____

5. From the tape, his wife thought he was smooth and confident.
   His wife is a very outgoing person.

   _____

   _____

6. Later, Barry confessed that he was really shy.
   Barry is an honest man.

   _____

   _____

7. His date eventually married him anyway.
   His date is also an honest person.

   _____

   _____

ANSWERS ARE ON PAGE 171.

Who and Which

———— Setting Your Thoughts Spinning ————

How can we combine these two sentences?

Jack Riley will handle your complaint.

Jack Riley has seen problems like this before.

We can write:

Jack Riley, **who has seen problems like this before,** will handle your complaint.

———— Pulling It All Together ————

We combined the sentences above by doing three things.

1. We substituted *who* for *Jack Riley* in the second sentence.

2. Then we took the phrase beginning with *who* and placed it inside the first sentence. We put the "who" phrase next to what it referred to, *Jack Riley.*

3. We used commas to set off the phrase beginning with *who.*

Words like *who* help us stick whole sentences inside other sentences. Other words like *who* that we will learn about in this chapter are *which* and *that.*

> *Who* is used to help identify or describe a person.

   Francesca spoke at our meeting.
+ She was invited by the lodge president.

= Francesca, **who was invited by the lodge president**, spoke at our meeting.

Who makes the sentence combination work by referring back to *Francesca.*

> *Which* is used to help identify or describe a thing.

   This cabinet is very well made.
+ This cabinet was donated by Miranda Suttles.

= This cabinet, **which was donated by Miranda Suttles**, was very well made.

So far we have used *who* or *which* to add description to the subjects of our sentences. We can also add description to other parts of the sentence.

1.   Jane called Barry.
+ Barry was very surprised.

= Jane called Barry, **who was very surprised.**

2.   I lent Fred my car.
+ My car was out of gas anyway.
= I lent Fred my car, **which was out of gas anyway**.

We can also add description to words following connectors like *to*, *from*, *for*, and others.

Terry got his jacket from the bus.
+ The bus had broken down on 5th Street.

= Terry got his jacket from the bus, **which had broken down on 5th Street**.

Working Out

This exercise provides practice in using *who* and *which*. Combine the following pairs of sentences. The cue card *someone* will signal you to look for someone to substitute the word *who* for. The cue card *something* will signal you to look for something to substitute the word *which* for. Remember to use commas to set off your "who" or "which" phrase. The first one is done for you.

LAKESIDE EDUCATION CENTER

1. I take courses at Lakeside Education Center.
Lakeside Education Center is for adults only.   something

   I take courses at Lakeside Education Center, which is for adults only.

2. Harry talked me into going with him.
Harry is a friend of mine.   someone

   _____
   _____

3. His brother didn't want to go.
His brother thinks he knows everything.   someone

   _____
   _____

4. I signed up for the GED class.
The GED class is held in the evenings.   something

   _____
   _____

5. Ron May signed me up for it.

Ron May knew Harry.   someone

_____

_____

6. I now have my high school diploma.

My high school diploma means a lot to me.   something

_____

_____

7. Now I'm taking their accounting class.

Their accounting class is offered only once a year.   something

_____

_____

8. Harry is taking a graphic arts class.

Harry always signs up for something.   someone

_____

_____

9. These adults can benefit by taking night classes.

These adults are eager to learn.   someone

_____

_____

10. I have made many new friends.

They feel as I do about Lakeside.   someone

_____

_____

ANSWERS ARE ON PAGE 172.

On Your Own

Complete the following sentences with your own "who" or "which" construction. Don't forget the commas! The first one is done for you.

1. Math, *which was my worst subject,*
   always made me nervous.

2. That teacher _____
   taught me more than anyone else.

3. This adult education class _____
   _____ was the most beneficial.

4. _____, who _____
   _____ was my best
   friend in school.

5. Schools _____
   are not for everybody.

6. My job _____
   requires further training.

The Useful That

—————— Setting Your Thoughts Spinning ——————

Look at these two sentences:

> The train arrives at 4:05.
>
> It will take you to Belmont Station.

Is there a way to combine them without worrying about commas? Is there a way to combine them without worrying about matching up the proper connecting word (*who* or *which*)?

> The train **that** will take you to Belmont Station arrives at 4:05.

—————— Pulling It All Together ——————

That is a useful connecting word because it can be used with both people and things. It can also be used to help describe different parts of your sentences. In addition, it never needs commas.

In the example in Setting Your Thoughts Spinning, we used *that* to combine sentences to describe a subject, *the train*. We used *that* to replace the subject in the second sentence, *it*. Both *it* and *that* referred back to *the train*. The word *that* enabled us to stick the second sentence inside the first.

You can also use *that* to help describe other nouns in a sentence. For example:

>   Frank has a difficult job.
> + It wears him out.
>
> = Frank has a difficult job **that** wears him out.

Using *that* can add description to words following connectors like *to*, *from*, and *for*.

>   I got this coupon from the newspaper.
> + The newspaper was on the table.
>
> = I got this coupon from the newspaper **that** was on the table.

Working Out

Combine the following sentences using the word *that*. The first one is done for you.

A SUPER HOUSEKEEPER

1. Estelle is a housekeeper.

   A housekeeper takes pride in her work.

   Estelle is a housekeeper that takes pride in her work.

2. After her husband had retired, Estelle wanted a job.

   A job would provide extra money.

   _____

   _____

3. A newspaper was all she needed.

   A newspaper had "part-time help wanted" ads.

   _____

   _____

4. The bus was late.

   She took the bus to her first interview.

   _____

   _____

5. The home was in a friendly neighborhood.

   She would clean this home.

   _____

   _____

6. Estelle was hired by the husband and wife.

   The husband and wife interviewed her.

   _____

   _____

7. She organized an entire household.

   The household really needed her.

   _____

   _____

ANSWERS ARE ON PAGE 172.

More about Time

———— Setting Your Thoughts Spinning ————

Look at the two sentences below. Each describes an action. Can these sentences be combined?

> The children started to throw candy.

> We left the movie theater.

You can use **time words** to combine sentences that show different actions. For example, here we combine the two sentences above:

> **When** the children started to throw candy, we left the movie theater.

—————— Pulling It All Together ——————

There are several words you can use to join sentences by showing time. *When* and *whenever* are two such words. For example:

> I finally relax.

> The telephone rings.

> **Whenever** I finally relax, the telephone rings.

Notice that, when the time word comes at the beginning of the sentence, you need to use a comma before the second part of the sentence. Now look at the same sentence reversed.

> The telephone rings **whenever** I finally relax.

As you can see, no comma is used if the time word is in the middle of the sentence.

The time words *when, whenever, as,* and *while* are used to join sentences when both actions are happening at the same time.

For example:

> Frankie lay groaning.
> + I took his temperature.

> = **As** Frankie lay groaning, I took his temperature.

The time words *after* and *before* can show which of two actions came first.

For example:

>   The game ended.
>   + Matt and Cedric stopped for a beer.
>
>   = After the game ended, Matt and Cedric stopped for
>   a beer.

From this sentence, you know that <u>first</u> the game ended and <u>then</u> the men stopped for a beer. Which action came first in the following sentences?

>   We sat in the park in total darkness.
>
>   The sun rose.

Since the action in the first sentence must have come first, we can combine the sentences like this:

>   We sat in the park in total darkness **before** the sun
>   rose.
>
>   OR
>
>   **Before** the sun rose, we sat in the park in total
>   darkness.

Working Out

Combine the following sentences using time words. The cue cards on the right tell you which time word will make the most sense in the sentence. Remember to use commas where needed. The first one is done for you.

THE BILTMORE AVENUE LAUNDROMAT

1. I go to the Laundromat. | Whenever |
My palms sweat.

Whenever I go to the Laundromat, my palms sweat.

2. I get there. | Before |
I'm already tired from sorting and packing clothes.

_____

_____

3. I arrive. | When |
The attendant starts giving me a hard time.

_____

_____

4. I'm getting change.   As
   She's complaining that I'm using too many machines.

   _____

   _____

5. I pour the soap in.   While
   I wish for a new washing machine.

   _____

   _____

6. My old one broke.   After
   I had to go to the Biltmore Avenue Laundromat.

   _____

   _____

7. The washer stops.   When
   I have to fight for a dryer.

   _____

   _____

8. I jump over a laundry cart.   As
   The clothes I carry drip on the floor.

   _____

   _____

9. The attendant mops up after me.   While
   She complains about the mess I make.

   _____

   _____

10. My clothes are dry.   After
    I fold them and get out of there.

    _____

    _____

ANSWERS ARE ON PAGE 172.

On Your Own

Try rearranging some of the sentences you've just written so that no comma is necessary. You do this by moving the time word phrase to the end of the sentence instead of the front. Changing some sentences around will give your writing more variety.

2. _____

_____

3. _____

_____

4. _____

_____

5. _____

_____

6. _____

_____

7. _____

_____

8. _____

_____

9. _____

_____

10. _____

_____

Comparing and Contrasting

Setting Your Thoughts Spinning

What are these two cars like? How are they similar? How are they different? How would you write sentences to describe them?

Take a little time now to describe these two cars. Use some of the sentence-building techniques you've learned so far. Write a paragraph or two before you continue with this lesson.

Pulling It All Together

Sometimes your purpose for writing may be to compare or contrast two people, places, events, or ideas. To **compare** is to discuss what is <u>similar</u> about two things. To **contrast** is to talk about how two things are <u>different</u>.

Writing to compare and contrast is more than just listing the similarities and differences. Of course, you can start with jotting down lists. However, to give your reader a clear understanding of your topic, you'll want to write sentences and paragraphs. The sentence combining you've done in this chapter will help you do this.

Working Out

The writer of the following letter wanted to describe her two brothers. She thought a good way to describe how they were alike and how they were different would be to talk about the cars they drove. This writer used too many short, choppy sentences. Rewrite the letter on the lines below, using the words and skills you learned in this chapter, such as:

1. *both...and*
2. *and* and a comma to join two sentences
3. *but, yet,* or *however* to join sentences
4. appositives
5. *who, which,* or *that*

My brothers are a little hard to describe. Cal is much older than I am. Brian is younger. You can tell a lot about them from the cars they drive. Cal drives a station wagon. Cal is a family man. The car is not a new model at all. It is called a ranch wagon. Often, there are toys on the floor of the car. Often, the seats are sticky from the children's spilling soda pop.

Cal's family comes before his car. Brian loves his car more than anything. Brian owns a very classy car. Brian is the swinging single of the family. His car is a classic British model. The car has a steering wheel on the right, not the left.

Cal wants things to be practical. Brian wants things to be impressive. Cal knows quality when he sees it. Brian knows quality when he sees it. Most people admire Brian's car. Cal thinks it is too showy.

Brian wanted to live far from the city. Cal wanted to live far from the city as well. Brian found a country home in an exclusive suburb. He was determined to have the best of everything. Cal moved to a quiet little town. He was determined to care for his family.

My brothers are a little hard to describe.

_____

_____

_____

_____

_____

_____

_____

_____

_____

_____

_____

A SAMPLE PARAGRAPH IS ON PAGE 173.

On Your Own

Compare your revision of the letter with the original. Did you find different ways to combine sentences? Do you now see some variety in your sentences?

Now compare your revision with the one in the Answer Sampler. How could you improve your version? Could you have combined more sentences?

Closing the Chapter

———— You Have Learned That ————

1. you can combine whole sentences with words like *and*, *but*, *who*, *which*, and *that*.

2. you can use time words such as *before* and *while* to join sentences.

3. there is a wide variety of sentence patterns you can use to compare and contrast.

———— Review Exercise ————

For each sentence given below, choose a joining word from the chart. Use this word to add additional information to the sentence. The first one is done for you.

and	but	who	which	that	before	after
as	whenever	while	yet	however	when

1. My son sends me money each month.

My son sends me money each month, yet I still can't pay my bills.

2. I usually go shopping on Sunday.

_____

_____

3. This city needs more parks and playgrounds.

_____

_____

4. My friend really loves to go out dancing.

_____

_____

5. Writing is a useful skill to develop.

_____

_____

Chapter 7

Relating Ideas to Persuade or Explain

——————————— **Your Chapter Goals Are** ———————————

1. to learn to use
   - *since* and *because* to show reason
   - *so* and *therefore* to show result
   - *furthermore* and *moreover* to give additional information
   - *if* to show condition
   - *though* and *although* to show contradiction.
2. to practice writing a variety of sentences that persuade or explain.

It is always a challenge to explain why you have done something or why something happened. Have you ever had to explain why you took a job or quit a job? Have you ever explained how something works?

It is also a challenge to get people to accept your point of view. Have you ever had to give your reasons for believing something? Have you ever written a letter to the editor in a newspaper to take a side on an issue?

Writers use a variety of sentences to explain and persuade. This chapter will help you write some of these types of sentences.

The Reasons Why

—— Setting Your Thoughts Spinning ——

Child: "How come?"

Parent: "Because."

Child: "Because why?"

Parent: "Just because!"

We know from conversations like this one that *because* by itself does not give a reason. It is actually used to connect a reason to a result. Do you know any other words that are used in the same way as *because*?

—————— Pulling It All Together ——————

How could you combine these two sentences?

I went to the liquor store.

We had run out of beer.

Can you see that one action (*running out of beer*) is a <u>reason</u> for the other action? Can you also see that one action (*going to the liquor store*) is the <u>result</u> of the other action? How can you show this relationship in one sentence?

First try matching up reasons and results in the columns below.

Reason	Result
It was getting dark out.	We should care for our senior citizens.
She is the best candidate.	He spent hours reading the help wanted ads.
Beef is so expensive.	I plan to vote for her.
They are important members of society.	We moved the party inside.
Tom needed a new job.	My family eats a lot of chicken.

Now that you are getting an idea of the relationship between reasons and results, think about what words you could use to show this relationship in one sentence.

You have seen how to combine sentences with *and* and *but*. These words are used to show when ideas are similar or different. What words can we use to show <u>reason</u> and <u>result</u>?

> The connecting words *since* and *because* join a reason to a result in one sentence. Use a comma after the reason when it comes first in the sentence.

Try combining the following sentences using the above rule. To help you get started, write *reason* and *result* next to the sentence each applies to.

The protective seal had been broken. _____

Mr. Montoya would not buy the aspirin. _____

_____

_____

Were you able to see that the first sentence is the reason and that the second is the result? You can combine these sentences two ways:

Because the protective seal had been broken, Mr. Montoya would not buy the aspirin.

OR

Mr. Montoya would not buy the aspirin **because** the protective seal had been broken.

Of course, you can also use the connecting word *since* in place of *because*. Notice that when the reason (beginning with *because*) came first in the sentence, a comma was needed.

To make sure you get the idea of reason and result, try putting *since* or *because* in front of the wrong sentence. You would get something like this:

The protective seal was broken **since** Mr. Montoya would not buy the aspirin.

That doesn't make much sense, does it? If you ever have trouble deciding what is a reason and what is a result, try putting *since* or *because* in front of each sentence to see which makes sense.

> **Remember** that *since* or *because* is always attached to the reason.

Here are the simple formats for using these joining words:

> Since _____, _____.
>   *reason*   *result*
>
> Because _____, _____.
>   *reason*   *result*
>
> _____ since _____.
>   *result*   *reason*
>
> _____ because _____.
>   *result*   *reason*

Working Out

Dimitri is trying to get a group of neighbors together to clean up their streets and parks. He needs to give lots of reasons to convince people that he has a good idea.

Combine the following sentences using either *since* or *because*. Try to start some sentences with reasons and some with results. This will give variety to your writing. To help you get started, label each sentence either *reason* or *result* in the space provided.

Remember to use a comma when the reason comes first. Also remember that *since* or *because* should always be attached to the reason. When you've finished combining the sentences, you'll have sentences for a useful handout that Dimitri could pass out to his neighbors. The first one is done for you.

1. We should take more pride in what is around us. *result*

   This is our home. *reason*

   Since this is our home, we should take more pride in what is around us.

2. The streets and sidewalks are covered with litter. _____

   Our neighborhood is neither pretty nor safe. _____

   _____

   _____

3. There is a lot of work to be done here. _____

   We need as many people as possible to help out. _____

   _____

   _____

4. Everyone should participate in a cleanup day. _____

   Everyone will benefit from a cleaner place to live. _____

   _____

   _____

5. We are planning to divide into two different groups. _____

   The work will go more smoothly that way. _____

   _____

   _____

6. Weekends are most convenient for everyone involved. _____

Saturday and Sunday will be Neighborhood Cleanup Days.

_____

_____

_____

ANSWERS ARE ON PAGE 173.

——————————————— **On Your Own** ———————————————

Think of something that you believe in strongly. It could be anything from your feelings about a movie you just saw to a political issue. Write five sentences telling someone why he should agree with you. Use either *since* or *because* in each sentence.

What's the Result?

—— Setting Your Thoughts Spinning ——

Look at the two sentences below and see if you can tell how one is related to the other.

> Vince thought he was underpaid.
>
> He asked his supervisor for a pay raise.

You may have figured out that you could combine these sentences with *since* or *because*, as in the last lesson. Do you know any other connecting words you can use to join these ideas?

—————— Pulling It All Together ——————

If you look again at the two sentences above, you may be able to see that the second sentence is the result of the first sentence. The example below gives you another way to show result in a sentence.

> Vince thought he was underpaid, **so** he asked his supervisor for a raise.

> *So* can connect two sentences to show a reason and a result. You must put a comma before the word *so*.

Read the two sentences below and label one reason and one result. Then combine the sentences using a comma and *so*.

> We extended lunch break to one hour. _____
>
> A half hour was not enough. _____
>
> _____

Can you see that the <u>reason</u> is that a half hour was not enough and that the <u>result</u> is that we extended the lunch hour? Here is the combined sentence:

> A half hour was not enough, **so** we extended lunch break to one hour.

Another good connecting word that shows result is *therefore*. It means the same thing as *so*, and we use both to add variety to our writing. Here's an example of sentence combining using *therefore*.

> We need more lights on our street.
> + We should ask our representative to request them.
> = We need more lights on our street; **therefore**, we should ask our representative to request them.

> *Therefore* can connect two sentences to show reason and result. You need to put a semicolon (;) before *therefore* and a comma after it.

You may remember that this punctuation was also used with the connecting word *however* in Chapter 6.

Read the two sentences below and write *reason* next to one and *result* next to the other. Then combine the two sentences using *therefore*.

Proper medical care is important for
newborns. _____

We should make sure new mothers are well
informed. _____

_____

Here is a simple way to remember the format of sentences that show reason and result:

> _____, so _____.
>   *reason*   *result*
> _____; therefore, _____.
>   *reason*   *result*

—————————————— **Working Out** ——————————————

Combine the following pairs of sentences. First, decide what connecting word you will use (*so, therefore, since,* or *because*) and write it in the blank cue card. The sentences are labeled reason or result to help you in your work. You will have sentences for a newspaper article when you have finished combining. The first one is done for you.

BUS ROUTE FOR THE DISABLED

1. **REASON:** The mayor called a city meeting to discuss public transportation cutbacks.
   RESULT: Many people from the city gathered at city hall. ┌─────────┐ *Since* └─────────┘

Since the mayor called a city meeting to discuss public transportation cutbacks, many people from the city gathered at city hall.

2. **REASON:** The Alliance of the Disabled was not pleased with the present transportation system.
   RESULT: It planned to insist on a new bus route for the disabled. ┌─────────┐ └─────────┘

_____

_____

3. **_REASON:_**   The alliance is a very well-known lobby
           group.
     RESULT: Its presentation got plenty of media
           coverage.   ☐

_____

_____

4. **_REASON:_**   The alliance speeches were clear and
           forceful.
     RESULT: The Transportation Board listened carefully.   ☐

_____

_____

5. **_REASON:_**   Getting on and off regular buses is a
           problem for these people.
     RESULT: Special service is needed for them to get
           around.   ☐

_____

_____

6. **_REASON:_**   The disabled have an equal right to public
           services.
     RESULT: Without special buses, their rights are being
           denied.   ☐

_____

_____

7. **_REASON:_**   The board said that city tax revenues were
           down.
     RESULT: Cutbacks were needed to make ends meet.   ☐

_____

_____

8. **_REASON:_**   Finally, the mayor decided that the rights of
           the disabled were most important.
     RESULT: The new bus service was approved.   ☐

_____

_____

COMPARE YOUR ANSWERS WITH THOSE ON PAGE 174.

On Your Own

Below you are given either a reason or a result. You are also asked to add one or the other. Then combine the two sentences using *so*, *therefore*, *because*, or *since*. The first one is done for you.

1. *REASON:* I like to sleep a lot.

   RESULT: _I usually am late for work._

   COMBINED SENTENCE: _I usually am late for work because I like to sleep a lot._

2. *RESULT:* Luella is never on time for work.

   REASON: _____

   COMBINED SENTENCE: _____

   _____

3. *REASON:* We believe the new tax plan is unfair to the poor.

   RESULT: _____

   COMBINED SENTENCE: _____

   _____

4. *REASON:* I dislike my job.

   RESULT: _____

   COMBINED SENTENCE: _____

   _____

5. *RESULT:* The man fell down the sewer.

   REASON: _____

   COMBINED SENTENCE: _____

   _____

Giving More Information

——— Setting Your Thoughts Spinning ———

Sometimes you may want to add information to a sentence. As you know, you can use *and* to do this. If you used *and* to combine all your ideas, however, your writing would get repetitive and boring. What are some other words you could use to give more information in a sentence?

——————— Pulling It All Together ———————

The joining words *moreover* and *furthermore* will help you. Here is an example of sentence combining using one of these connectors.

        The judge took bribes.
    +   He failed to file an income tax return last year.

    =   The judge took bribes; **moreover,** he failed to file an
            income tax return last year.

Both *furthermore* and *moreover* mean "in addition." Using one of these words can add emphasis to your point. Instead of giving long lists of ideas in your writing, you can combine them with these words. They can put more variety into your sentences.

Notice that a semicolon and a comma are used just as they were with *therefore*. The format to remember for this type of sentence is:

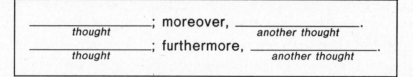

Remember that the two thoughts or ideas you join must be complete sentences on their own. For example:

Don't write: We need more money for the project;
                furthermore, more manpower.

Write: We need more money for the project;
        furthermore, we need more manpower.

If you are not sure whether you can use *moreover* or *furthermore* to join two ideas, try using *and*. If *and* makes sense, the other two joining words will as well. Can you join these sentences with *furthermore* or *moreover*?

    My favorite sport is baseball.

    I can get bored playing it.

Try using *and* to join them:

> My favorite sport is baseball, **and** I can get bored
> playing it.

Can you see that this doesn't make much sense? These sentences would be better combined with *but* since they are showing different ideas. Therefore, don't use *furthermore* or *moreover* to join these ideas.

—————————— Working Out ——————————

Some sentences are started for you below. Add an additional idea to each one, using either *furthermore* or *moreover*. Make sure that your ideas make sense joined in this way. Sometimes you'll have to fill in a blank with your own words first. The first one is done for you.

1. A friend of mine sometimes gets on my nerves.

   A friend of mine sometimes gets on my nerves; furthermore, she can be a pain in the neck.

2. Addison broke his arm in the car accident.

   _____

   _____

3. I usually spend my evenings at _____.

   _____

   _____

4. A skill I really found valuable to learn is _____.

   _____

   _____

5. My goals in life sometimes seem _____.

   _____

   _____

6. One thing that really drives me crazy is _____.

   _____

   _____

SOME POSSIBLE SENTENCES ARE ON PAGE 174.

What If . . .?

—— Setting Your Thoughts Spinning ——

What kind of sentences are used to show what is needed to get a certain result? What sentences are used to predict what will happen as a result of something else?

A **conditional** sentence tells you what needs to take place in order for something else to take place. In other words, this type of sentence shows you when one idea <u>depends</u> upon another. Here is an example:

If we keep spending money, we'll be broke soon.

The <u>condition</u> in this sentence is *if we keep spending money*. What will happen, or the <u>result</u>, is that *we'll be broke soon*.

—— Pulling It All Together ——

The connecting word *if* can be used to join two sentences in order to show a condition and a result. If the condition comes first in the sentence, a comma must be placed before the result.

Try combining these two sentences using the rule above.

Condition: Carl needs a ride.
Result: Tyrone will drive him to the station.

_____

Suppose we don't know whether the first sentence is true or not. In other words, we are unsure of whether Carl needs a ride. Therefore, we combine the sentences like this:

If Carl needs a ride, Tyrone will drive him to the station.

OR

Tyrone will drive him to the station **if** Carl needs a ride.

Some writers like to include the word *then* in the result part of their conditional sentences. For example:

If Carl needs a ride, **then** Tyrone will drive him to the station.

Working Out

Below you are given either a condition or a result. You are also asked to add one or the other. Then combine the two sentences using **if**. The first one is done for you.

1. *CONDITION:* Our country keeps building nuclear weapons.

   RESULT: *We may have another world war.*

   COMBINED SENTENCE: *If our country keeps building nuclear weapons, we may have another world war.*

2. **RESULT:** Mrs. Dantis will keep gaining more and more weight.

   CONDITION: _____

   COMBINED SENTENCE: _____

   _____

3. *RESULT:* I will learn more about the world and its people.

   CONDITION: _____

   COMBINED SENTENCE: _____

   _____

4. **CONDITION:** You keep yelling at me like that.

   RESULT: _____

   COMBINED SENTENCE: _____

   _____

5. *CONDITION:* I can put away enough money this month.

   RESULT: _____

   COMBINED SENTENCE: _____

   _____

6. **RESULT:** People will think I'm very funny.

   CONDITION: _____

   COMBINED SENTENCE: _____

   _____

SOME SAMPLE SENTENCES ARE ON PAGE 174.

In Spite Of

———— Setting Your Thoughts Spinning ————

When was the last time you thought of a reason not to do something but then did it anyway? For example, have you ever been on a diet and then had an ice cream sundae anyway? Have you ever wanted to get to work early and then slept late instead?

People contradict themselves all the time. A **contradiction** exists when someone says something, then does the opposite. Write down something you have done lately in spite of reasons not to. Then write down a reason not to do it.

What I did:

Reason not to do it:

———— Pulling It All Together ————

Writing to explain or persuade can be difficult because of contradictions. Luckily, we have words and sentence structures to help us. You have already learned about *but* and *however*, which can help to show contradictions. Now learn two more connecting words.

> The connecting words *though* and *although* can be used to join two sentences to show contradiction. If the connecting word comes first in the sentence, put a comma between the two parts of the new sentence.

Try connecting the two ideas you wrote above using *though* or *although*. They both mean the same thing, so use either one. For example:

  Wendell voted for the Republican candidate.
+ He has always been a Democrat.

= Wendell voted for the Republican candidate
   although he has always been a Democrat.

OR

Although he has always been a Democrat, Wendell
voted for the Republican candidate.

Notice that a comma is needed only when the connecting word comes first in the sentence. Can you see that Wendell <u>had a reason</u> not to vote for a Republican but he did it anyway?

Working Out

Part A

Sometimes it is hard to tell when something is a contradiction. See if you can match each action in the left column with the correct contradiction in the right column. Write the appropriate letter next to each sentence in the left column. One of them is done for you.

1. Seth bought a new tie. *C*

2. We chose a new insurance plan. _____

3. The band played on Thursday. _____

4. Sometimes people can't sleep. _____

5. Capital punishment is fair. _____

6. We should elect Mrs. Lloyd. _____

a. They were scheduled for Friday.

b. She has little experience.

c. He had no need for one.

d. They are tired and run-down.

e. We liked the old one.

f. It is taking another's life.

Part B

Now that you have matched up the contradictions, combine each pair using *though* or *although*. Remember to use a comma when the connecting word comes first in a sentence.

THE COMBINED SENTENCES ARE ON PAGE 175.

On Your Own

Complete the following sentences with your own ideas. Then, on the line below, rewrite each sentence with the connecting word at the beginning of the sentence. Remember the comma! The first one is done for you.

1. My favorite food is spaghetti though *it is fattening.*
   Though it is fattening, my favorite food is spaghetti.

2. I enjoy going to school although _____

   _____

3. I spend a lot of time worrying although _____

   _____

4. Television is entertaining though _____

   _____

Persuading Your Reader

—— Setting Your Thoughts Spinning ——

You may already know that the Statue of Liberty, a symbol of freedom for Americans, is badly in need of repair. People from all across the nation are being asked to give money to make the statue beautiful again.

For a long time, the Statue of Liberty has attracted tourists to New York City. Should only the people of New York pay to have it fixed? Or do you think that the statue belongs to all Americans and that all should contribute?

Some people say that New Yorkers make lots of money from having the statue as a tourist attraction. These people think New York should pay to repair it. Other people say that the statue is a symbol of national pride. These people think it is the duty of all Americans to restore the statue.

Take some time now to write down your opinion about this. Tell who you think should pay and why. Try to use different kinds of sentences in your work.

Pulling It All Together

When you write to persuade someone, you want to be as convincing as possible. You want to give your reader good reasons to see your point of view. The types of sentences you have learned in this chapter should help you do this.

A letter to the editor is one example of persuasive writing. A person writes to a newspaper to give her opinion on an issue. She hopes that readers of the newspaper will agree with her point of view.

Working Out

Fran Mulligan wrote the following letter to the editor of her town newspaper. She wanted to convince the people of Baytown to contribute to the Statue of Liberty fund. Rewrite Fran's letter so that it is more persuasive. Use the following sentence combining techniques to make the ideas more clear.

1. *since* or *because* to show reason
2. *so* or *therefore* to show result
3. *moreover* and *furthermore* to show additional ideas
4. *if* to show when one idea depends on another
5. *though* and *although* to show contradiction

Dear Editor:

The Statue of Liberty needs a lot of repair. Many people from across the country are donating money. Some citizens of Baytown do not want to help pay for the repair. They agree that the statue is a mess.

These citizens feel that only New York benefits from the statue. It is a tourist attraction there. New Yorkers enjoy the statue. They should pay for its repair. The citizens of New York let the statue decay in the first place. They did nothing about it for years.

I respect the people of Baytown. I disagree with them. The Statue of Liberty was a gift to all Americans. We are all responsible for it. We continue to let it fall apart. Other countries will think we have lost our pride as a nation.

Extra money is scarce these days. We can all donate to this worthy cause. We restore our national symbol. We can be proud of our country.

AN IMPROVED LETTER IS ON PAGE 175.

Closing the Chapter

——————— You Have Learned ———————

1. how to use certain words to relate ideas in sentences.
2. how to construct sentences that explain or persuade.
3. how to increase the length and variety of your sentences.

——————— Chapter Review Exercise ———————

For each sentence given below, choose one connecting word from the chart. Use this connecting word to lengthen the sentence. The first one is done for you.

because	since	so	therefore	moreover
furthermore	if	though	although	

1. We need more supplies for this project.
   We need more supplies for this project if we want to do it correctly.

2. I really like to eat out on weekends.

   _____

   _____

3. Our country does not care for all of its citizens.

   _____

   _____

4. We will end up with plenty of money.

   _____

   _____

5. People who steal from others should be punished.

   _____

   _____

Chapter 8
Writing for a Purpose

———— Your Chapter Goals Are ————

1. to practice informative, persuasive, and descriptive writing.

2. to examine sentences used by professional writers.

3. to practice using sentence constructions you have learned in this book.

The lessons in this chapter will give you some chances to write for different purposes. You will write to inform your reader, persuade your reader, and describe something to your reader. You will be able to use many of the sentence building ideas you've learned so far.

You will also have a chance to see how other writers use different sentence structures. By looking closely at their writing, you will see that there are many, many ways to express ideas. You will see that professional writers use many of the same types of sentences you use, as well as others.

Just the Facts, Ma'am

Writing a News Article

In this lesson, you'll write a news article about a concert that took place in your town. The band could be your favorite group. It could be a rock band, a rhythm and blues group, or any other kind of musical group. Your job is to <u>inform</u> readers of what went on at the concert.

Some Helpful Hints

Newspaper articles give facts about people, places, and events. They tell *who, what, when, why,* and *where.* News articles do not have sentences that start with *I think* or *In my opinion.* This is because, in newspaper reporting, facts are important, not the writer's opinion.

To help you get started writing your article, fill in the blanks below. This will give you the information, or facts, that you need to start writing your article. Use your imagination.

Who? _____

What? _____

Where? _____

When? _____

Why? _____

Now put these facts into sentences. Of course, you'll want to include other ideas and facts in your article. For instance, what songs did the band play? What did the band look like? How was the weather?

Now write your news article on a separate piece of paper. Make it ten or fifteen sentences long and really try to let the reader know what the concert was like.

——————————— Working Out ———————————

Below are some sentences taken from a news article about a concert. Combine these sentences using techniques you learned in this book. Use whatever way you think sounds best. Put your new sentences in paragraph form. When you are done, turn to the Answer Sampler. There you will find another writer's article made from the same sentences.

{The Tower Theater in Philadelphia was the scene of an old time rock and roll party.
{The Tower Theater was sold out.

{It was February 13, and people had come to hear the British soul of Wham!
{It was a Saturday night.

{Wham! features two talented young men.
{Wham! is the latest musical import from Great Britain.

{These handsome men gave the audience ninety minutes of song and entertainment.
{These handsome men are George Michael and Andrew Ridgeley.

{The audience got 100% Wham!.
{They got 100% all night.

{Wham! wanted its first American tour to be special.
{It wanted its first American tour to be exciting.

{The band chose to play only in medium-size concert halls.
{People filled the halls every time.

{The Tower Theater was a perfect place to stop.
{The Tower Theater has a long history of rock and soul.

TURN TO PAGE 176 TO SEE HOW ONE REPORTER WROTE THE ARTICLE.

Vote!

———— Writing a Letter to the Editor ————

Would you vote for a woman for vice president? How could you convince other people to do the same? In this lesson, you'll have a chance to write a persuasive paragraph. In it, you will give your point of view on having a woman vice president. You will also give the reader reasons to think the same way you do.

———————— Some Helpful Hints ————————

Here are some ideas that may help you get started writing your letter.

1. Decide what your opinion is first and write it down somewhere. Write it in a complete sentence, such as "I do not think a woman should be vice president" or "Women should be able to become vice president."

2. Make a list of all your reasons for your point of view. Try to think of good reasons that will convince your reader. Then write down some reasons why someone might disagree with you.

3. Make sentences from your ideas. Try to use the techniques you learned in Chapter 7. For example:

> A woman should not be able to become vice president **because** women have not had much experience in government.

OR

> **Although** a woman has never been vice president before, this doesn't mean women are not qualified.

4. As you write, keep in mind questions that someone might have about your opinion. Keep your ideas convincing.

5. Write your paragraph as a letter to the editor. Remember that letters to the editor appear in newspapers and magazines. They represent readers' opinions on all kinds of topics. Finish writing your letter before you go on to the next activity.

_____

_____

_____

_____

_____

Working Out

In 1984, for the first time in history, a woman was nominated to run for vice president of the United States. In her speech accepting the nomination, Geraldine Ferraro wanted to persuade people to vote for her and her running mate. By combining the sentences below, you will come up with parts of her speech. Some of your sentences may be a little different from the way Ms. Ferraro wrote them. This is OK. Just compare your answers with the Answer Sampler. You may be surprised to see how similar your writing is to hers.

Choose a connecting word from the box below to join each pair of sentences. Try to choose the one that you think makes the most sense.

| if   and   when   because |

1. I became an assistant district attorney.
   I put my share of criminals behind bars.

   _____

   _____

2. You obey the law.
   You should be protected.

   _____

   _____

3. I first ran for Congress.
   All the political experts said a Democrat could not win in my
       home district of Queens.

   _____

   _____

4. We are going to win.
   Americans across this country believe in the same basic dream.

   _____

   _____

5. We can do this.
   We can do anything.

   _____

   _____

6. Our own faith is strong.

We will fight to preserve the freedom of faith for others.

_____

_____

7. Let no one doubt that we will defend America's security around
the world.

Let no one doubt that we will defend the cause of freedom
around the world.

_____

_____

8. We leave our children nothing else.

Let us leave them this earth as we found it—whole and green
and full of life.

_____

_____

*TURN TO PAGE 176 TO SEE HOW THESE
SENTENCES WERE ACTUALLY WRITTEN.*

————————————— **On Your Own** —————————————

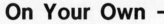

Stop by your public library and ask a librarian to help you find copies of some political speeches. Read one or two of them and look closely at the kinds of sentences used. Judge for yourself how persuasive the writer is.

Describing in Detail

Writing a Description

Look at this picture. Where is this scene? What time of day is it? Who is the owner of the boat? Why is it docked here? Why are there no people in sight? In this lesson, you'll have a chance to describe this scene in any way you'd like. You will let your imagination go and use lots of specific details to describe it.

Some Helpful Hints

If you are having trouble thinking of what to write, try the brainstorming technique you learned in Chapter 1. Write down any words or phrases that come to mind when you look at the picture. Use these ideas to come up with words that describe the scene.

Now put these ideas into sentences. Try to use some of the techniques of combining that you learned in this book. Remember that the more detail you add to your sentences, the better your reader will understand you.

Try to write at least fifteen sentences about the picture. Do this before you go on to the next exercise.

Working Out

Ernest Hemingway, a well-known writer, described many scenes like this boat scene in his book *The Old Man and the Sea*. By combining the sentences below, you will come up with many of the same sentences Hemingway wrote in this book. Use the cue card provided to join each pair of sentences. Remember to use correct punctuation.

1. There was no one to help him.

He pulled the boat up as far as he could.   so

_____

_____

2. His left hand was still cramped.

He was unknotting it slowly.   but

_____

_____

3. The sun was hot now.

The breeze was rising gently.   although

_____

_____

4. He knew quite well the pattern of what could happen.

He reached the inner part of the current.   when

_____

_____

5. The fish had slowed again.

The fish was going at its usual pace.   and

_____

_____

6. The sun had gone down.

He had been in the fight with the sharks.   while

_____

_____

*TURN TO THE ANSWER SAMPLER ON PAGE 176
AND COMPARE YOUR ANSWERS TO THESE.*

Another Chance to Persuade

Giving Your Opinion

You have the right to believe whatever you want. Your opinion belongs to you, and it is never "wrong." Of course, it helps to know some facts before you make up your mind. An informed opinion is always better than one formed without thinking.

Do you think this country should have a national holiday in honor of Dr. Martin Luther King, Jr., or President John F. Kennedy? Think about it for a minute. How would you persuade someone to agree with your opinion on this issue?

Some Helpful Hints

If you are having trouble making up your mind about this issue, perhaps some facts will help you form an opinion.

- Americans celebrate the birthdays of important people in United States history (such as President Washington and President Lincoln) with a national holiday.

- Some states have already declared January 15 as Martin Luther King, Jr., Day.

- John F. Kennedy was a president both respected and admired until his assassination in 1963.

- Martin Luther King, Jr., was a champion of equal rights, and his teachings became the model of the civil rights movement in the sixties.

- Some employers feel that we already get enough days off. Others feel strongly that we need a special day to remember the people who have influenced our lives.

With these ideas in mind, write a short paragraph telling how you feel about creating a national holiday to honor one or both of these men. Make sure you state your opinion strongly! Give reasons for your point of view.

_____

_____

_____

_____

_____

_____

_____

Working Out

Read the paragraph below. It is taken from a very famous speech made by Martin Luther King, Jr. If you look carefully, you will see that Dr. King uses some of the same sentence constructions that you have learned to use. He also uses some different ones. This paragraph can give you an idea of the endless number of ways sentences can be made. The more you write, the more of these types of sentences you will be able to use.

Answer the questions after reading the passage. By doing this activity, you will become more aware of language and how people use it in their writing.

> I say to you today, my friends, so even though we face the difficulties of today and tomorrow, I still have a dream. It is a dream deeply rooted in the American dream. I have a dream that one day this nation will rise up and live out the true meaning of its creed. "We hold these truths to be self-evident, that all men are created equal." I have a dream that one day on the red hills of Georgia, sons of former slaves and the sons of former slave owners will be able to sit down together at the table of brotherhood. I have a dream that one day even the state of Mississippi, a state sweltering with the heat of injustice, sweltering with the heat of oppression, will be transformed into an oasis of freedom and justice. I have a dream that my four little children will one day live in a nation where they will not be judged by the color of their skin but by the content of their character.

1. In Chapter 4, you saw that sometimes repetition can hurt your writing and sometimes it can help it. Find the phrase that is repeated often in this speech.

   Write it here: _____

   Is it a repetition that hurts the passage, or does it emphasize what the writer and speaker feels is important?

2. Find the sentence referring to Mississippi. You may remember that the construction used here is called an appositive. What two ideas were combined to make this sentence?

   a. _____

   _____

   b. _____

   _____

3. The last sentence of this paragraph has a different structure from what you have learned in this book. The writer used the phrases "not by . . . but by" to build a strong sentence. Try writing one of your own with a little help. Fill in your own ideas.

> I have a dream that my children will one day live in a nation
>
> where they will not be judged by _____
>
> but by _____.

4. Notice the contradiction that Dr. King states in his first sentence. You learned in Chapter 7 that the word *though* can show what someone does in spite of a reason not to. What is Dr. King saying that he has? He has this in spite of what conditions?

WHAT HE HAS: _____

REASON NOT TO: _____

_____

SEE PAGE 177 FOR ANSWERS.

On Your Own

Find a copy of Dr. King's "Letter from Birmingham Jail." Again, ask your librarian for help in finding it. Read the letter and try to pick out the kinds of sentences you have learned to write. Then, take some time to look closely at new sentence patterns. Try writing sentences of your own using these patterns, as you did in #3 above.

Closing the Chapter

——————————— You Have Learned ———————————

1. that you know many sentence patterns that professional writers and speakers use.

2. that there is an endless variety of sentence patterns available to you as a writer.

——————————— An Optional Activity ———————————

You have seen in this chapter that you can learn a lot by reading good writing. Pick up a book, magazine, or newspaper, and take some time to look closely at the sentences a writer uses. Look for sentence patterns that you have learned already and jot them down in your notebook. Then find a couple of sentence patterns that are unfamiliar to you. Try writing some sentences of your own using these new patterns.

Section III:
Repairing

Chapter 9
Editing Your Work

────────── **Your Chapter Goals Are:** ──────────

1. to find out what you need to learn about proofreading and editing.

2. to take a first look at a system for editing your writing.

3. to review what makes up a sentence and to learn when to pull sentences apart.

Writing is work. But you don't have to do all your work at once. Every sentence you put down on paper for the first time does not have to be perfect. You should think up your sentences, get them down on paper, and worry about fixing them later.

Make sure, however, that you do work on them later. You've already seen how sentences can be improved by combining. You already know to go back over your sentences to see if you have enough variety. Now you have a third thing to do.

Writing mistakes, the kind you make when you are concentrating on the meaning of your words, need to be fixed. This "fixing" step is called **editing.** Editing is really just correcting your work so that it can easily be understood by a reader. The next four chapters will help you learn to edit your own writing.

There are lots of different mistakes writers make in their work. There is not enough room in this book to talk about every one of these mistakes. Instead, we will talk about the most common ones and the ones that harm your writing the most.

To Edit or Not to Edit

—————— Setting Your Thoughts Spinning ——————

What does editing look like? When you have finished a piece of writing, how do you go about fixing it? How can you tell what needs to be fixed and what doesn't?

——————————— Pulling It All Together ———————————

Fixing your own writing can be hard because you know what you are trying to say. Therefore, it's hard to pick out mistakes. For this reason, it is always a good idea to let your work sit for a while before you edit it. Try to leave it for a day or at least a couple of hours. In this way, you'll be reading it with a fresh mind.

Then what? Read your work over carefully and slowly. Make changes in words and spelling. Make sure you are using the words you intended to use. Make sure your sentences are complete. The next four chapters will tell you some specific things to look for in your writing.

Don't be afraid to mark up your own work! Use a different-color pen so you can see your changes clearly. Use cross-outs, arrows, and circles—anything that helps you see your mistakes clearly. Remember that what you first put on paper is not the final version of your writing. You are free to make all kinds of changes.

Below is an example of one writer's edited work. Notice the marks used. A (∧) means "insert" or "put in here." A slash (/) through a capital letter means to make it a small letter. When a word is crossed out, another word can be written above it.

I always ~~has~~ ^have^ to take a long tim^e^ to edit work. Sometimes I writ^e^ so fast that I dont notice What I am doing ^w^rong.

Working Out

How much do you already know about the correct way to write things? Try out your editing skills in this exercise. Cross out any mistakes and correct them like the sample above. Don't worry if you don't find all the mistakes. The next chapters will help you.

AN ANNOUNCEMENT

The Comunity Youth Center have started it's own Little League team! The team is for boys and girls 9-12 years of age. Living in the Mercino Park area. Players will be selected on a first come / first served basis but if enough youngsters apply, a second team will be formed.

The Community Council and Coach Pat Stern is handling applications. The child must be healthy, available for practice, and has to be able to get along with other kids, Equipment will be supplied by the center. Uniforms too.

Some games will be played across town. Pat Stern and me will take the team to these games in the center's bus. Pat a former junior high coach is the perfect chaperone

Register on Saturday morning, 12:00 until 3:00, in the lobby of the center, practice begins the following Saturday at 8:30.

THE EDITED VERSION IS ON PAGES 178-79.

Trick of the Trade

When you proofread something for the final time, keep a dictionary handy. Look up any word you have some doubt about. Keep a list of words that you misspell often.

What Is Not a Sentence

—— Setting Your Thoughts Spinning ——

A group of words can begin with a capital letter and end with a period but still not be a sentence. It may be a **sentence fragment.** A fragment, no matter how long, is missing something that would make it a sentence.

You learned about incomplete sentences in the first chapter of this book. Why are we discussing them again? We emphasize the problem of incomplete sentences because it is a common problem for writers. It is also a problem that can really harm your writing.

—————— Pulling It All Together ——————

To review, a complete sentence

1. does not leave you hanging. A group of words like *When they get home from work* leaves you hanging. You don't know what will happen *when they get home from work.*

2. has a subject. A subject tells *who* or *what* is doing an action. It can also tell *who* or *what* is being described.

3. has a verb. It can have an action verb like *does, followed,* or *drove.* Or, it can have a linking verb like *was, are, is,* and *looks.*

A sentence must have all three of these things. If you don't have all three, you have a fragment.

Editing your own writing for fragments can be difficult. It is easier when you follow these steps below.

1. Make sure you read each of your sentences one at a time.

2. Start with the capital letter and look for your subject and verb.

3. Read to the period and stop. Could this sentence stand alone? Is it really part of another sentence? Was anything missing?

You can also recognize fragments by remembering how you combine sentences. Words like *although, when, before,* and *because* connect sentences. The part beginning with one of these words should never stand alone. For example:

Error: Fred will ask her out. **Although** he'd rather date her sister.

No error: Fred will ask her out **although** he'd rather date her sister.

Also watch out for *-ing* words. For example:

> **Error:** Carlos didn't enjoy it. **Living** on a shoestring like
> that.

> **No error:** Carlos didn't enjoy **living** on a shoestring like
> that.

Once found, a fragment can easily be fixed by connecting it to the sentence it belongs with or by supplying the missing subject or verb.

———————————————— Working Out ————————————————

Edit the following letter, looking for sentence fragments. Combine a sentence with a fragment or supply a missing subject or verb.

WHAT ABOUT THE RENT?

Dear Mr. Craft:

I live in your Woodstock Building. On 52nd Street. Mr. Ronnie Counts is our building manager. Mr. Counts has informed me that my rent is more than five days overdue. He said I could be evicted. If I don't pay within two weeks.

I don't believe I should be harassed. By Mr. Counts. I have never been late before. Did tell him ahead of time about this month. You see, I changed jobs. My other employer paid me every two weeks. No final check from him yet. My new employer pays me once a month on the fifteenth. I have not received my first check from him yet. Because I am a new employee.

I explained this to Mr. Counts. I will pay my rent. As soon as I can. Would you tell Mr. Counts not to harass me unnecessarily? Thank you.

> Sincerely,
>
> Sylvia Levine

THE EDITED LETTER IS ON PAGE 179.

Pulling Sentences Apart

—— Setting Your Thoughts Spinning ——

When does a sentence stop? Which of these sentences didn't know when to stop?

a. He knows I am going away he doesn't care at all.

b. I enjoy creative projects, needlepoint has always been a favorite hobby of mine.

c. Whenever Fred wanted to call home, he had to find a pay phone.

—————— Pulling It All Together ——————

Sometimes we string too many sentences together into one long sentence. Once in a while we fail to connect sentences correctly. Both kinds of mistakes create **run-on sentences**.

When checking for run-on sentences:

1. Read each of your sentences from the capital letter to the period. Are there too many ideas in that sentence? Is there more than one complete thought without punctuation or a joining word? Look at **a** above. Can you see that there are two ideas run together here?

2. Look out for sentences stuck together with a comma and no connecting word. Commas cannot connect sentences by themselves. Words like *and*, *or*, *but*, and *so* are used with commas to connect sentences, as you learned in Chapter 6. Look at **b** above. Can you see that a joining word like *and* is needed here?

If you come across a run-on in your writing, don't panic. Run-ons can easily be fixed. One way is to pull the run-on apart and make two sentences. For example:

Run-on: He knows I am going away he doesn't care at all.

Fixed: He knows I am going away. He doesn't care at all.

Another way to fix run-ons is to use one of the connecting words you have learned in this book.

Run-on: I enjoy creative projects, needlepoint has always
been a favorite hobby of mine.

Fixed: I enjoy creative projects, **and** needlepoint has
always been a favorite hobby of mine.

Sentence C is not a run-on because it uses the joining word *whenever* to combine two ideas. Notice also that a comma is placed between the two ideas being joined.

Working Out

Practice editing for run-ons. Fix each run-on by either pulling the separate sentences apart or inserting connecting words.

THE CITIZENS BAND RADIO

I never would have bought a CB radio for myself, Harry said I needed one. We had just moved out to the country I had to drive forty miles to work. The drive was miles of woods and cornfields, and Harry was worried something might happen. At first I was shy about the CB, I hardly used it. My handle was "Buttercup," that didn't sound tough enough. I got into the habit of listening to truck drivers. From them, I got to know all the speed traps. I enjoyed their slang and secret messages. I never radioed any of them, I couldn't think of anything to say. One cold winter night I was on my way home from work. I heard a noise the car went out of control. I got control I found myself in a ditch on the side of the road. My CB was still working, I radioed for help. Finally a trucker's voice came over the radio he asked me where I was. I told him, and he said he would radio for a tow truck. I was saved!

THE EDITED PARAGRAPH IS ON PAGES 179-80.

Closing the Chapter

——————— You Have Learned ———————

1. that you should always look over your work and edit to get rid of mistakes.

2. to check your writing for sentence fragments.

3. to make sure to pull apart your run-on sentences.

——————— Summary Exercise ———————

Edit the following letter for fragments and run-ons.

Ms. Danita Lopes
Total Care Insurance Company
573 Huron Avenue
Cleveland, Ohio 42356

Dear Ms. Lopes:

We spoke on the telephone Wednesday. About discontinuing my health insurance. I thought the price for individual coverage was too high I couldn't afford it. I was discontinuing my group plan.

My employer informed me that my group coverage will end in thirty days. Because I am leaving my job. Although I didn't want the coverage when we last talked. I have decided to pick it up after the thirty days are past.

Please send me the necessary forms, thank you for your help on the telephone. Please send me a new list of participating clinics in my area they will be helpful to me.

Sincerely,
Rick Listenbee

Chapter 10

Everything in Its Place

──────── **Your Chapter Goals Are:** ────────

1. to be able to locate and fix problems with pronouns.

2. to be able to locate and fix problems with describing words and comparisons.

3. to remember to check your sentences to see if everything is in the right place.

In English, certain words are used only at certain times. We generally have a sense that this is so whether we remember the specific rules or not. That's why people make a point of correcting children. If they say, "Mary and me are going outside," we say, "Mary and I."

In this chapter, you will learn about words that are used only in certain ways. You will learn to spot when one of these words is not used correctly.

Problems with Personal Pronouns

—— Setting Your Thoughts Spinning ——

Pronouns are words that take the place of nouns. For instance, we can use the word *it* to substitute for the name of any object.

Noun: Maurice folded **the newspaper** in half.

Pronoun: Maurice folded **it** in half.

Personal pronouns are words like *I, me, she, he, it,* and *my.* Many personal pronouns change their form when their use in a sentence is changed. For instance, *he* and *him* are different forms of the pronoun that refers to a man. Depending on where it is used in a sentence, either *he* or *him* may be correct.

How familiar are you with the rules for using words like *he* and *him* correctly? Circle any mistakes in the sentences below.

Rowena and her sold tickets to the church social.

Maxie saw Mark and I at the drugstore.

—— Pulling It All Together ——

In this lesson, we will concentrate on the confusion between pronouns that can be the subjects of sentences and pronouns that cannot be subjects.

can be subject	never subject
I we you they he she it	me them us him her

To decide what pronoun to use, ask yourself if your pronoun will be the subject of a verb. If so, you will use a pronoun from the first column.

Paul said _____ watched the game on TV.

The Sweenys brought _____ a quart of ice cream.

What pronouns can you use in the blanks? Ask yourself if the pronoun will be the subject of a verb. In the first sentence the pronoun will be the subject of *watched.* Therefore, you should fill in a pronoun from the first column. In the second sentence the pronoun will not be the subject of a verb, so you must use one from the second column.

People often get confused when using *and* to join pronouns. Asking yourself whether your pronoun is a subject will help you with this problem. For example:

Write: Margaret and **he** will pick you up at eight.

Don't write: Margaret and **him** will pick you up at eight.

Since the pronoun is part of the subject of the verb *will pick,* you must use a pronoun from the first column not the second. Sometimes it helps to cross out the noun and *and* that are joined to the pronoun. For example, cross out *Margaret and.* Now read the rest of the sentence. Would you say *He will pick you up at eight* or *Him will pick you up at eight*? Try this one yourself. Which pronoun in parentheses is correct?

Mark asked Eugene and (I, me) to help him study for the apprenticeship test.

You might be tempted to choose *I* because it sounds right. However, ask yourself if the pronoun is the subject of any verb in the sentence. Since it is not, you should choose *me.* For another test, try crossing out *Eugene and.* Would you say *Mark asked I to help him study* or *Mark asked me to help him study*?

Working Out

Practice editing to make sure you've used the correct pronoun. Cross out each error you find and write the correct form above it.

A LETTER OF REFERENCE

Dear Mr. Brooks:

I hear that Ivan Petrovich and his wife have applied for an apartment in our building. My wife Rosa and me have known them for years. We met Olga and he shortly after they came to the United States. We have been fast friends ever since.

They were also the best neighbors we ever had. Ivan and me work at the same factory. Olga and him both have steady jobs and are never late with the rent. They even helped Rosa and I when I was out of work.

Bob, I would appreciate it if you would do this favor for Rosa and I. Please approve the Petroviches' application. You won't regret it.

Sincerely,

Miguel Solis

THE EDITED LETTER IS ON PAGE 180.

Words that Describe

——— Setting Your Thoughts Spinning ———

Look at the dark-type word in each of the sentences below. What kind of information does each word give? Does it tell you what someone or something is like? Or does it tell you how something was done?

> He walked **slowly** away from the wrecked car.

> The **slow** car was hit from behind.

——————— Pulling It All Together ———————

There are two kinds of describing words you have used in this book. One kind describes people, places, or things in sentences. These are words like *pretty*, *tough*, or *weird*. These words, as you saw in Chapter 2, are called **adjectives**. The other kind of describing word tells you more about an action. These words tell where, when, how, or how much and are called **adverbs**. Some adverbs are *quickly*, *very*, and *poorly*. If you want a review of this kind of describing word, turn back to the lesson on pages 16-17.

Many adverbs are close in form to an adjective, except that they end in *-ly*. Sometimes this leads to confusion about which word should be used when. For instance, do you run out of money *quick* or *quickly*? Should you describe a party as *exciting* or *excitingly*? The basic rule is:

> Adjectives describe nouns. Adverbs describe verbs.

Here are some extra hints to help you make the right choice between adjectives and adverbs.

1. Adjectives are used with being verbs. These are forms of *to be* (*is*, *are*, *were*, etc.), *taste*, *stay*, *look*, *sound*, *feel*, *become*, *appear*, and *grow*.

    > The house looks **different** somehow.

    > That tastes **strange** to me.

2. Adverbs are used with action verbs. These are words like *hit*, *drive*, *sell*, *work*, and others.

    > I bet you will do that **differently** the next time.

    > The waitress looked at us **strangely**.

3. Adverbs also are used with adjectives and other adverbs.

    > Roberto felt **really** bad yesterday.
    > (*not* <u>*real*</u> *bad*)

    > Phoebe is **awfully** good at her job.
    > (*not* <u>*awful*</u> *good*)

Working Out

Practice proofreading for adjective/adverb mistakes. Cross out each error in the letter below and write the correct form above it.

February 19, 1985

Dear Aunt Benita,

It has been an awful long time since we've seen you. We hope you are well and real happy in your new apartment.

Our daughter Molly is five now. She is a good girl and plays quiet in the yard by herself. However, she can be bad sometimes. Yesterday I heard a sudden, loudly crash. I quickly ran to the kitchen. I couldn't see Molly anywhere.

I went to the back door and eager looked about the yard. There she was, under the kitchen window, loud banging together two garbage can covers. "Was I being bad?" she asked with a twinkle in her eye. I just had to laugh at her little joke.

Anyway, expect to see us at the family reunion this summer. We won't miss you so terrible if we have something to look forward to.

Your niece,

Gwen

THE EDITED NOTE IS ON PAGES 180-81.

On Your Own

In the chart below are some commonly confused adjective/adverb pairs. Use each word on the chart in a sentence. Altogether, you will write ten sentences. Check these sentences to see if you used each adjective and adverb correctly.

Adjectives	Adverbs
soft	softly
loud	loudly
good	well
bad	badly
careful	carefully

Misplaced Words

———— Setting Your Thoughts Spinning ————

What's wrong with these sentences? Do they make sense?

> I saw a wounded dog jogging along the highway.

> While walking through the woods, my foot got caught in
> some branches.

———— Pulling It All Together ————

Do wounded dogs jog?

In the first sentence the words *jogging along the highway* are misplaced. They are misplaced because they were meant to describe *I* and not
dog. Therefore, the phrase should be placed closer to *I*.

> Jogging along the highway, I saw a wounded dog.

It is very important that you place describing words close to the word they
modify. For example:

Misplaced:	The woman described the mugging at the police station.
Correct:	At the police station, the woman described the mugging.
Misplaced:	I bought a used car from a new dealership that was in mint condition.
Correct:	I bought a used car that was in mint condition from a new dealership.

Watch out for adverbs such as *almost, only, just, even, hardly, nearly,*
and *merely.* Put these in front of the word they describe. Notice how each of
these sentences means something different depending on where the describing word is placed.

> Paul said that **only** he would bet on the next race.
> *(Paul is the only one that's going to bet.)*

> Paul said that he would bet **only** on the next race.
> *(Paul is going to bet only on one race.)*

> Paul said **only** that he would bet on the next race.
> *(That is the only thing Paul said.)*

Misplacing words is one problem. Forgetting them entirely is another.

> While walking through the woods, my foot got caught in
> some branches.

A foot can't walk through the woods. There are two ways to fix a sentence
like this. One way would be to figure out what words are missing and add

them. Who was actually doing the walking? Add *I was* to the first part of the sentence.

> While **I was** walking through the woods, my foot got
> caught in some branches.

The other way to fix it would be to put the missing word *I* in the second part of the sentence. You may also have to shift around some additional words.

> While walking through the woods, **I caught** my foot in
> some branches.

—————————————— Working Out ——————————————

Read this letter carefully. Some sentences have misplaced describing words. Others are confusing because of missing words. Circle the misplaced words and draw an arrow showing where they belong. Insert any missing words.

Dear Senator Waters:

I am writing to give testimony that would ensure funding for alternative schools in support of Senate Bill HB 24371.

After dropping out of high school, things went from bad to worse. Because of not finishing high school, the world of work had no place for me. I was the last hired and the first fired. I could get jobs that paid only minimum wage. I fought with my bosses not knowing how to behave.

Wanting to get my act together, Monroe Alternative School was the place for me. I finished my high school education and took job orientation classes. I didn't have to worry about fitting in. I am now enrolled in a first-rate technical school setting my sights on a career in computer programming.

Dropouts have rights too. They have the right to a second chance. Second chances are cheaper than long unemployment lines. Please vote for HB 24371.

Sincerely,
Jeffrey Wilkins

THE EDITED LETTER IS ON PAGE 181.

Closing the Chapter

——————————— You Have Learned ———————————

1. to make sure you have used the correct pronoun in your writing.
2. to make sure you used the right describing word.
3. to check your writing to see that describing words and phrases are in the right place.

——————————— A Final Exercise ———————————

Choose a piece of writing that you did in a previous chapter. Try to pick one that has at least eight sentences. Now edit your work, paying particular attention to the four points above.

Chapter 11
Everything Must Match

──────── **Your Chapter Goals Are** ────────

1. to be able to put the correct verb with your subjects.

2. to be able to match pronouns with the words they refer to.

3. to use constructions that are parallel.

In writing, there are times when we have to make sure that certain words match. You already did some matching when you were reminded to put singular subjects with singular verbs in Chapter 1. You also learned that plural verbs go with subjects joined by *and*.

In this chapter, you will review the matching rules you have already used and learn some new ones as well.

Matching Subjects to Verbs

—— Setting Your Thoughts Spinning ——

How much do you remember about matching subjects to verbs? Match each subject on the left with a verb on the right. Some of the subjects may match up with the same verbs.

Subjects	Verbs
Maria, Carmen, and Luis	was exercising
Mona or her two sisters	am exercising
I	were exercising
Thom or Linda	

—— Pulling It All Together ——

Remember that singular subjects take singular verbs. Unless the subject is *I* or *you*, most verbs ending in a single *s* (*is, was, has, thinks, owns*) are singular. Plural subjects take plural verbs (*are, were, have, think, own*).

> **Singular:** The **truck was** loaded down with dirt and gravel.

> **Plural:** The **trucks were** loaded down with dirt and gravel.

Always watch out for words and phrases that come between the subject and the verb. Make sure your verb matches the subject, not the word closest to the verb. For example:

> **Don't write:** The neon **signs** on top of the building **was** burned out.

> **Write:** The neon **signs** on top of the building **were** burned out.

Can you see that *signs* is the subject of the verb *was burned*, not *building*? It was the *signs* that were burned out, not the *building*.

Remember that subjects joined by *and* are plural and therefore take plural verbs. For example:

> **Don't write:** The walls and the ceiling was painted.

> **Write:** The walls and the ceiling **were** painted.

When you join subjects with *or*, however, match the verb with the closest subject. For example:

> **Don't write:** The lawyers or the judge are wrong.
>
> **Write:** The lawyers or the **judge is** wrong.
>
> **Write:** The judge or the **lawyers are** wrong.

Can you see that, in the correct examples, the verb matches the subject closest to it?

─────────────────────── **Working Out** ───────────────────────

Edit the following political bulletin. Cross out the mistakes in subject-verb agreement and write in the correct verb above.

WHAT SHOULD CONGRESS WORK ON?

News reports about Congress has been a big disappointment this year. Congressional trips to Europe and the Far East is always being discussed. Who is paying for these trips? The IRS or the Government Accounting Office have to investigate these trips for the sake of American taxpayers.

The Senate and the House votes too much with the President these days. The branches of government is supposed to provide checks and balances against each other. So why do the President keep getting his MX missiles? Congress need to work harder to stop the arms race. It needs to provide a veto of the farm bill too. Many Congressmen were not even around for the vote. They were away on "business trips."

A new President or new members of Congress is needed to keep the public interest in mind. The votes of all citizens is needed to make sure this happens.

THE EDITED VERSION OF THIS LETTER IS ON PAGE 182.

Matching Pronouns

———— Setting Your Thoughts Spinning ————

Pronouns must match the words they refer to. Look at this sentence:

Ted raised his hand when he found the right answer.

His and *he* refer to back to *Ted*. The sentence wouldn't make much sense if you replaced *his* with *her* and *he* with *they*, would it?

———————— Pulling It All Together ————————

What word does each dark-type pronoun refer to?

The ministers wanted Tim to join **their** church.

Denny showed my wife **his** report card.

In the first sentence, *their* refers to *ministers*. This pronoun correctly matches the word it refers to. How do you know it doesn't refer to Tim? You know this because Tim is singular and would need a singular pronoun to replace it. In the second sentence, *his* refers back to *Denny*. You know it doesn't refer to wife because *his* refers to a male, not a female.

When checking to make sure your pronoun matches the word it is supposed to, decide what word that pronoun refers to. If you used a plural pronoun (such as *their* or *them*), make sure it refers to a plural word somewhere else in the sentence.

When nouns are joined by *and* or *or*, it can sometimes be tricky deciding on the correct pronoun to use in your sentence. Can you see how unclear the meaning is in this sentence?

Mark and Angelo brought his date to the party.

Whose date did they bring? Mark's? Angelo's? Or did they both bring dates? It is not clear to whom the pronoun *his* refers.

Only you, the writer, know what you mean to say. The sentence above can be made clear in different ways, depending on what the writer really meant.

Mark and Angelo brought Mark's date to the party.

Mark and Angelo brought Angelo's date to the party.

Mark and Angelo brought their dates to the party.

When you join two nouns with *or* or *either . . . or*, your pronoun should match the noun closest to it. For example:

Don't write: Either the Swains or Holly sent their reply.

Write: Either the Swains or **Holly** sent **her** reply.

Write: Either Holly or the **Swains** sent **their** reply.

Mistakes are often made when using pronouns like these:

each	one	somebody	anyone	neither	everyone
either	nobody	no one	someone	everybody	

Although some of these words seem plural in meaning, they are actually singular. An easy way to remember this is to look at their endings *(one, body)* and think of them as single units. Because they are singular, match them only with singular pronouns. For example:

Don't write: Somebody lost **their** lunch.

Write: Somebody lost **his** lunch.

Write: Somebody lost **her** lunch.

Sometimes a writer may not know whether to use a masculine or a feminine pronoun. If you are in this situation, don't just use the plural. Try to rewrite your sentence in a different way so that you won't need to use a pronoun.

Somebody lost a lunch.

Working Out

Edit the following memo, looking out for unmatched pronouns. Cross out any mistake and write the correct pronoun above it.

TO: Mr. Henry A. Goodson, Vice President

Each of us in the clerical pool wants their children in a day care center in the vicinity. Some of us travel for miles before and after work to pick up her children at nursery schools or baby-sitters' homes.

We regularly have to refuse overtime. Everyone of the clerks has gotten into trouble with their supervisor for lateness. Mr. Svec was reported to have mentioned several of us in their monthly report.

Many of our major companies today run its own day care centers. These centers are very profitable. Convenience and peace of mind have its benefits. Contented employees work harder. They also come in earlier and accept overtime.

Please look into this matter. Either we or our supervisor wants to get together with you about it soon.

THE EDITED MEMO IS ON PAGES 182-83.

Making Things Parallel

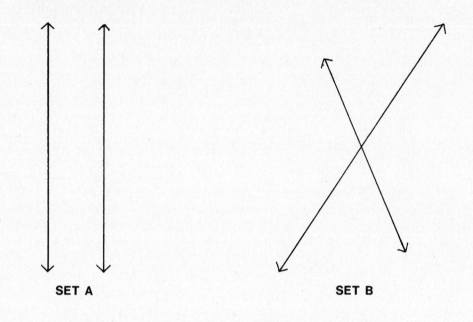

SET A   SET B

———— Setting Your Thoughts Spinning ————

What does the word *parallel* mean? Which set of lines is parallel?

The lines in Set A are parallel. They are parallel because they go in exactly the same directions. In English, words are parallel because they are formed the same way and are used for the same purpose. Which two of the following sentences have parallel expressions?

I dislike shopping for clothes and to exercise.

I dislike shopping for clothes and exercising.

———— Pulling It All Together ————

The words we put together to form sentences should match in certain ways. Words that we put together using *and* or *or* are supposed to be in the same form. This is especially true when we are making a series.

> The words joined by *and* or *or* should be all nouns, all verbs, all adjectives, all adverbs, or all phrases.

For example:

Don't write: Belinda is calm,   cool,   and a
                              adjective *adjective*

trustworthy person.
              noun

Write: Belinda is calm,   cool,   and trustworthy.
                        adjective *adjective*   *adjective*

Can you see that, in the correct sentence, all three words joined by *and* are adjectives? Here's another example:

Don't write: My daughter's favorite sports are <u>baseball</u>,
noun

<u>basketball</u>, and <u>playing</u> soccer.
    noun   *verb*

Write: My daughter's favorite sports are <u>baseball</u>,
                          noun

<u>basketball</u>, and <u>soccer</u>.
  noun   *noun*

Parallel structure is something that you should watch out for when combining sentences. For example, how would you combine the ideas in these two sentences?

Harry likes to travel.

He likes having new experiences.

Joining the sentences by just using *and* is not correct. For example:

Don't combine: Harry likes to travel and having new experiences.

Combine: Harry likes **to travel** and **to have** new experiences.

OR

Harry likes **traveling** and **having** new experiences.

Notice how you have to change one item to fit the other in form. Try combining the three sentences below, watching out for parallel structure.

Mayor Bell is planning to lower property taxes.

He is planning to improve public transportation.

He plans to reform city hall politics.

_____

_____

Remember that sometimes words have to be changed to fit the others in a series.

Don't combine: Mayor Bell is planning **to lower** property taxes, **to improve** public transportation, and **plans** to reform city hall politics.

Combine: Mayor Bell is planning to **lower** property taxes, **improve** public transportation, and **reform** city hall politics.

Working Out

Part A

Each sentence below contains two or three words joined by *and*. Label each word a noun, verb, adjective, or adverb. If a sentence does not have parallel form, rewrite it correctly on the line below it. The first one is done for you.

1. Darlene gets plenty of sound sleep, good food, and

   is taking high-powered vitamins.

   Darlene gets plenty of sound sleep, eats good food, and takes high-powered vitamins.

2. Tim didn't know whether to listen to the radio, the television,

   or play the stereo.

   _____

   _____

3. The restaurant serves pancakes, hamburgers, and has omelets.

   _____

   _____

4. Raoul's girlfriend is kind, affectionate, and has patience.

   _____

   _____

5. Stephanie opened the door slowly, carefully, and was fearful.

   _____

   _____

Part B

Edit this announcement about a day camp, watching out for parallel structure errors. Cross out any unmatched word or group of words. Write your change above the incorrect forms.

THE NEIGHBORHOOD CLUB DAY CAMP

Our new day camp will be fun, exciting, and can be enjoyed.
The children will need a vacation from school, and you will need
to vacation from them.

This year the kids will enjoy hiking, swimming, singing, and do
arts and crafts. You will get some free time and be having peace of
mind.

Contact Mindy for information about registration at 532-1616.

ANSWERS AND THE EDITED ANNOUNCEMENT ARE ON PAGE 183.

Closing the Chapter

——————— You Have Learned ———————

1. how to make sure your subjects and verbs match.
2. how to make sure your pronouns match.
3. how to make sure your words are parallel.

——————— Another Assignment ———————

Edit this note to the baby-sitter. Correct all errors.

Dear Susan,

Don and his wife is stopping by later to leave Tammy off. Let both girls play quietly in the living room until 8:30. Each of the girls should have their Barbie doll to play with.

There should be no eating candy, watching cable TV, or telephone calls for the girls. Make sure Debbie and Tammy brush her teeth, take her bath, and goes to bed at 9:00.

In case of an emergency, you can reach us at the Fredericks'. The emergency numbers for help is taped to the telephone.

Chapter 12

Problems with Punctuation

―――――――― **Your Chapter Goals Are** ――――――――

1. to learn to avoid confusion between contractions and pronouns that show ownership.

2. to review uses of commas and semicolons.

3. to learn more uses for commas.

There are many punctuation errors you can make when you write. This chapter deals with the most common ones.

Much of this chapter reviews comma and semicolon rules that you learned while combining sentences. Other comma rules concerning dates, direct address, and words coming at the beginning of sentences are also introduced.

The chapter begins with a lesson on confusing contractions and pronouns that show ownership.

Confusing Contractions

———— Setting Your Thoughts Spinning ————

Sometimes two words are combined into one. *Do not* can be *don't*. *It is* can be *it's*. These words are called **contractions**.

A contraction is formed by using an apostrophe. The apostrophe stands in for a letter or letters that have purposely been omitted.

———— Pulling It All Together ————

Some contractions are confusing because they sound like other words we know. It is easy to use these words in the wrong places.

Contractions	Words Showing Ownership
they're *(they are)*	their
who's *(who is)*	whose
it's *(it is)*	its
you're *(you are)*	your

Don't write: Their leaving a car with us during the summer.

Write: They're leaving a car with us during the summer.

Don't write: We were surprised that the stray cat found it's way back here.

Write: We were surprised that the stray cat found **its** way back here.

A good way to check yourself is to find every contraction you've used. Replace each one with the two words it stands for. See if the sentence still makes sense. For example:

You should wipe you're feet before coming into the house.

You should wipe (you are) feet before coming into the house.

The second sentence makes no sense at all. Therefore, use the word that shows ownership:

You should wipe **your** feet before coming into the house.

Another way to check your work is to find every word that shows ownership, such as *their, its,* and *your.* Replace each word with a phrase that means the same thing. (For example, *our car* means *the car belonging to us. Its face* means *the face belonging to it.*) See if the sentence still makes sense. For example, try the one below.

Your going to be a father.

Replace *your* with the phrase it stands for.

The going of you to be a father.

This makes no sense at all. Therefore, you should use a contraction in place of the word showing ownership.

You're going to be a father.

—— Working Out ——

Look for contractions or words showing ownership in the note below. Cross out each word that is used incorrectly. Then write the correct form above it.

From the desk of

Kim Pyun

You're letter of resignation caught me by surprise. Its always a difficult thing to lose a good employee. This is especially true with someone who's work has been as good as yours.

Your welcome to come by the office before you leave. I hear you're men are giving you a going-away party. Their going to miss you. You've been they're supervisor for a number of years now.

Good luck at Beckwith Brothers in California. Its a great company, and your going to love the climate.

THE EDITED NOTE IS ON PAGE 184.

Commas, Semicolons, and Sentence Combining

─── Setting Your Thoughts Spinning ───

In Chapters 5-7 you learned many ways to combine sentences. Some methods for combining sentences required you to use commas or semicolons. This lesson will give you a brief review of these uses.

─── Pulling It All Together ───

1. When making a series using *and* or *or*, make sure you have a comma between items in the list.

>   Melanie will be attending.
> +   Paulette will be attending.
> +   Ann will be attending.
>
> =   **Melanie, Paulette, and Ann** will be attending.

2. When forming appositives, make sure you set the appositive off with commas.

>   Trixie Doyle was a mobster's girlfriend.
> +   Trixie Doyle was a character in a movie.
>
> =   Trixie Doyle, **a character in a movie**, was a
>   mobster's girlfriend.

3. Make sure you put a comma after the first part of a sentence you began with one of the following words:

> | | | |
> |---|---|---|
> | before | although | because |
> | after | though | when | since |
> | if | as | while |

>   Reggie came late.
> +   He still wanted to see the rest of the hockey game.
>
> =   **Although Reggie came late,** he still wanted to see
>   the rest of the hockey game.

4. When you sometimes use *who* or *which* to add information to a sentence, set off the part beginning with *who* or *which* with commas.

>   The mayor was tired of answering questions.
> +   He held a press conference earlier.
>
> =   The mayor, **who held a press conference earlier,**
>   was tired of answering questions.

5. Remember to use a comma before *and, but, or,* or *so* to join two complete sentences.

> Tracy wanted to visit her grandmother.   but
> + She had to stop by the clinic first.
>
> = Tracy wanted to visit her grandmother, **but** she had to stop by the clinic first.

There is one way you have learned to use semicolons.

> Put a semicolon before *therefore, however, furthermore,* and *moreover* when using these words to combine sentences. Remember to put a comma after each as well.

> Ron was two weeks late in completing a construction project.
> + Demoting him from foreman was a fair decision.
>
> = Ron was two weeks late in completing a construction project; **therefore,** demoting him from foreman was a fair decision.

——— Working Out ———

Edit this letter for punctuation. Add any commas or semicolons that may have been left out. Cross out any unnecessary commas.

Dear Mr. O'Geara:

Winter is over and it is time to start repairing potholes. My neighbor, who is a clerk in the records department told me an interesting fact. Although, our neighborhood draws some tourist trade our streets have been repaired only three times.

Because the potholes are now quite big I suggest you get your workers, over here soon. The streets, have flooded badly this spring so you may need to work, on the sewers as well.

Our block club will be having a meeting, on Sunday. You are invited to come. We are really very angry about the condition of our streets moreover we intend to write the mayor.

Sincerely,

Roberto Duff

THE EDITED LETTER IS ON PAGE 184.

Some Places for Commas

———— Setting Your Thoughts Spinning ————

In writing, we use commas to group words. We do this to break up long and involved sentences so our readers can understand them better. We also use commas to make it clearer how our ideas are connected. In this lesson you'll learn some different ways to use commas.

Don't forget that too many commas can be just as confusing as too few. Use a comma only when there is a specific reason to do so. Whenever possible, you should let sentences flow without stopping the reader. Look at the sentence below. See how unnecessary commas make it hard to read.

> Stacy, and Crystal, can leave for school, as soon as, I
> find Stacy's book report.

———————— Pulling It All Together ————————

Let's first look at how commas can make writing easier to read and understand. Does the sentence below make sense to you?

> On April 14 1982 Matt and I met I believe at the Old
> North Church.

This is a case where commas can help the reader know when to pause. Here is the sentence with the commas placed correctly.

> On April 14, 1982, Matt and I met, I believe, at the Old
> North Church.

There are rules for when and where to place commas to help your reader. We will discuss them here.

> Use commas to set off words of **direct address.** Words of direct address identify whom we are speaking or writing to.

Don't write: This Ms. Howard is my final warning.

Write: This, **Ms. Howard,** is my final warning.

Ms. Howard is the name of the person being spoken to. Therefore, we put a comma before and after her name to set it off.

> Use commas to set off any words or groups of words not essential to the meaning of your sentence.

These are usually interrupters like *well, of course, as a matter of fact, by the way*, and others. For example:

> **Don't write:** Stephen Spielberg as a matter of fact directed *Close Encounters of the Third Kind*.

> **Write:** Stephen Spielberg, **as a matter of fact,** directed *Close Encounters of the Third Kind*.

> Use a comma after any word or group of words that introduces the rest of the sentence.

Introducers are words or phrases that come before the subject and the verb of a sentence, such as *however, well, at the shop, before noon*, and *others*. For example:

> **Don't write:** However lower taxes should be a campaign issue.

> **Write: However**, lower taxes should be a campaign issue.

> **Don't write:** In the event of a blackout have a flashlight handy.

> **Write: In the event of a blackout,** have a flashlight handy.

> Use commas to separate certain parts of addresses and dates written in sentences.

In an address, make sure you separate the street, the town or city, and the state. Do not separate the street number from the street or the state from the zip code. For example:

> **Don't write:** Mail this letter to Lucia Alvarez 6923 Dolton Avenue Taos New Mexico 87359.

> **Write:** Mail this letter to Lucia Alvarez, 6923 Dolton Avenue, Taos, New Mexico 87359.

In a date, put a comma between the day and year, but not between the month and day. You will also need a comma after the year to separate it from the rest of the sentence. For example:

> **Don't write:** I was drafted on August 8 1969 in the middle of the Viet Nam War.

> **Write:** I was drafted on August 8, 1969, in the middle of the Viet Nam War.

Working Out

Add the commas to this announcement where necessary. Cross out any unnecessary commas. Remember, unless you have a specific reason for using a comma, it probably doesn't belong there.

FREE HEALTH EDUCATION LECTURE

On Tuesday evening March 24 1986 we will be offering a free, health education lecture. Our guest speaker, back by popular demand will be Dr. Helen Fairchild Curreros.

The lecture will be held, at the City-Wide Adult Education Center 1411 West Fourth Street Houston, Texas 41173. By the way you can write to the center for further information, and a list of future programs.

Ladies it's important that you, and your loved ones attend this lecture. Dr. Curreros will be discussing the seven, warning signs of cancer. Moreover she will discuss how fear is cancer's best friend.

East Texas Women's Society

THE EDITED ANNOUNCEMENT IS ON PAGE 184.

Trick of the Trade

The greeting in a personal letter is punctuated differently from the greeting in a business letter. Here is an example:

Business: Dear Ms. Banta:

Personal: Dear Sheila,

Notice that a comma is used only after the greeting of a personal letter.

On Your Own

Below is a review exercise where you can practice editing for all kinds of comma and semicolon errors. Cross out each error and insert the correct punctuation marks wherever necessary.

TAMPA—Late Friday afternoon a Delta DC-10, crashed just after takeoff from the Tampa International Airport. No serious injuries were reported but at least 100 passengers were treated for minor burns, and smoke inhalation.

Passengers included vacationers businesspeople and several new crew members, in the Delta training program. Most were able to continue their travel on other carriers, however, some were held in a nearby hospital overnight.

Although considerable investigation was done at the crash site no explanation for the accident has been announced. However a press conference, will be held later today at the Tampa airport.

Closing the Chapter

───────── You Have Learned ─────────

1. how to avoid confusion between contractions and possessive forms of pronouns.
2. how commas are used to separate extra words and ideas in sentences.
3. how commas and semicolons are used with sentence combining.

───────── Summary Exercise ─────────

Edit this letter, correcting any errors in punctuation.

Dear Mr. Ryan:

You're delivery service leaves something to be desired. Most of the time, my newspaper isn't even delivered. When it is I often find it in the bushes, or in my neighbor's yard. You're paper boy needs to be reminded who's paper he is delivering. And I might add he also needs throwing lessons.

You always bill me, for full service; whether I receive it or not. So if the service does not improve I will drop delivery altogether.

Enclosed; is partial payment for last month.

Sincerely

Joan Bennett

An
Answer
Sampler

Section I Answers

Chapter 1
Introducing Sentences

page 5 ————————————— **Working Out** —————————————

Remember that this is just a sample of what you could have written.

First Mother: "I sure waited a long time for this bus."

Second Mother: "So did I. The service seems to get worse every day."

First Mother: "You would think they could get enough decent buses in a city this size."

Second Mother: "I agree. Once I waited an hour for a bus on Seattle Street. Then it broke down two blocks up the street!"

First Mother: "The drivers are sure nice, but these buses have seen better days!"

Second Mother: "Yeah. It makes you want to walk or buy a car."

First Mother: "For sure!"

pages 7-9 ————————————— **Working Out** —————————————

Part A

1. b   3. a

2. d   4. c

Part B

Of course, your answers may be different because you would say something different. Compare your ideas to these.

1. When will it start feeling numb?
   to ask a question

2. Pass the salt and pepper, please.
   to give a command

3. You'll get dirty if you go outside.
   to give information

4. What is the new fare?
   to ask a question

Part C

1. Will the dentist give novocaine?
   Give me a shot of novocaine.

2. Will you pass the salt and pepper?
   Pass the salt and pepper.

3. Are you getting ready to go?
   Get ready to go!

4. Are you going to get on this bus?
   Get on this bus.

5. Do you understand that we love you?
   Understand that we love you.

——————— **Working Out** ———————   page 11

You probably added different words to make sentences. Use these sentences below as models to compare your work to. Do all your sentences have subjects and verbs?

2. **The woman** spoke quietly to the manager.

3. **She** had long black hair and wore heavy eye makeup.

4. The elderly manager **asked her to take a seat next to the white screen**.

5. **A handsome man** was sitting behind a white screen.

6. Angry and annoyed, he **threw a bucket of water over the screen**.

7. Finally, the two people **got up and stormed out**.

8. **They** laughed about it later.

——————— **Working Out** ———————   page 13

Are all of your sentences complete thoughts like the model sentences below?

2. **They took the express bus** so that they would not be late.

3. If my boss would just leave me alone, **I could get some work done around here**.

4. When Kingsford saw them coming, **he headed in the other direction**.

5. **We wanted to finish our cookout** before the sun went down.

6. **Dick said he robbed the store** because he needed the money.

7. After Dawn took the test, **she had a big party at her house.**

8. **We ordered a deluxe pizza** since we all like sausages.

page 15 ———————————— **Working Out** ————————————

You may have described these actions differently. That's OK. Compare your work to the work below. Did you use lots of different action words? Notice that the writer also included other actions that he visualized himself.

> The victims of the boating accident **screamed** loudly for help until finally two policemen **rushed** to the scene. The embankment was steep, so both officers **clung** tightly to rope that was safely **secured** above. As they **edged** down toward the water, one officer **leaned over** and **hurled** the rope to the closer victim. This man **reached** desperately for line. Meanwhile, a woman barely **held** herself above water a short distance from the embankment. She **stretched** one arm high over her head to **signal** for help.

page 17 ———————————— **Working Out** ————————————

Your when, where, and how words will be different. Use the paragraph below to compare with your work.

> The scene at the pub last night was really wild. A stranger **casually** walked in and **immediately** ordered a beer. **Suddenly**, the regular customers realized that they had seen the man **before**. He was the one who had gotten into a fight **over** at Nell's Disco the other night. They looked at him **angrily** and then **loudly** asked him to leave. **Soon**, a huge brawl broke out **everywhere** in the place. **Finally** the police arrived and **quickly** broke up the fight.

Chapter 2

A Chance to Describe Something

page 21 ———————————— **Working Out** ————————————

2. action
3. description
4. action
5. action

6. description
7. description
8. action

page 23 ———————————— **Working Out** ————————————

Your description will probably be very different from this one. Read this model over carefully and notice all the describing sentences. Did you use sentences like these in your work?

> Plain rock and roll is my favorite music. Bruce Springsteen is the best singer around. His songs are sometimes slow and sad and sometimes loud and fast. He is always entertaining on stage. Springsteen is a good performer because he sounds exciting every time I hear him. Unlike punk rock, his music will remain popular forever.

Working Out
pages 25-27

Part A

You probably used different describing words. That's OK. Try to check your work against this model to see if you used good describing words too.

Last night I turned my **new** television set to the **late** news. It was time for the weather report. A **cheerful** weatherman was doing the report this time. He said a **huge** blizzard was expected. Our **little** city would get **two feet** of snow? I couldn't believe it. We have already had a **horrible** winter. Next year I'm moving to **sunny** Florida.

Part B

Carla works for a **twenty-four hour** answering service. She works the **long and boring** night shift. The building, **creaky and old**, is deserted. One night she had quite a **frightening** experience. First she heard the **squeaky** elevator doors open. Then she heard **loud** footsteps. Carla grabbed a **heavy, marble** paperweight. She ran for the **open** door. Whack! She looked down at the body of her **unconscious boyfriend** on the floor.

Working Out
page 29

Use the model below to compare with your work. Did you use lots of describing words and sentences?

I am an Aquarius, and I am very intelligent. Most people I know think I am smooth and interesting, but I think I am often dull and awkward. People with my sign are supposed to be talkative and loud. I have actually always been quiet and shy. Someday I will be a nurse and will do the things I am best at. I enjoy caring for people and making sure they are happy. Maybe I am not like other Aquarius people, but I like who I am.

Chapter 3
Timing Your Sentences

Working Out
page 33

2. The mail **takes** a long time to get here!

3. We **are using** the expressway to get to work.

4. Hank **is enjoying** his new Cadillac more than ever.

5. I **learn** all kinds of new skills at work.

6. Jesse **looks** really sharp these days.

7. As usual, the race **ends** before midnight.

8. You **are trying** very hard on tests, Bill.

pages 34-35
Working Out

Part A

Make sure that all verbs are in the past tense like those below.

The rocky hill **overlooked** the riverfront. The meeting **was scheduled** for midnight. It **was** lonely up on that hill. Looking down at the riverfront, Jake Blaine **noticed** two headlights. They **were making** their way among the maze of warehouses and piers to the foot of the hill. The headlights **were cut off.** Jake **heard** car doors slam. Two men **began** to climb the hill.

Part B

Your letter will probably be different. Look at the paragraph below and notice all the future tenses used. Did you use future tense in your letter?

My story **will be** great. It **will be** complete soon, I think. It **will be** a story about a murder near the river in Oakton. It **will be** published in July. The characters **will be** realistic, but the story **will be** fiction. I think you **will** really **enjoy** reading it.

page 37
Working Out

Part A

The process for writing a business letter is very simple. **First**, you must find clean stationery and a good pen. **Second**, put the date and your home address at the top right-hand corner of the paper. **Next**, skip a couple of lines and, at the left margin, write the name and address of the person you are writing. Begin your letter a couple of lines underneath with "Dear So and So." **Then**, skip another couple of lines and begin the body of the letter. **Next**, close your letter with a phrase such as "Sincerely yours." **Finally**, sign your name and print it underneath.

Part B

Your ideas and paragraph will be a lot different from these. Make sure you used lots of time words to help your reader.

PICNIC

fry chicken	buy hamburger meat	pack food
make desserts	pack up car	start fire on grill
set up picnic table	put meat on grill	relax for a while
play games or read	serve meal	clean up

We've had so many picnics that they get easier and easier to plan. **First**, I always fry chicken ahead of time. **Then** I buy plenty of hamburger meat for the whole crowd. **Third**, I make desserts and pack up all the food in a crate and cooler. **After** we pack up the car, we head for the picnic grounds. **Next**, we set up the picnic table and start the fire on the grill. **Then** we relax a while. We play games or read **while** the meat cooks. **Finally**, it is time to eat, and I serve the meal. **Last**, we all clean up and go home.

Chapter 4
Watching Your Words
———— Working Out ————   page 41

Of course, your ideas are probably a lot different. You probably wrote a very different paragraph too. That's OK. Use the ideas and paragraph below to compare with what you have written.

Part A

bride	scared
groom	quiet
ceremony	short
weather	hot
reception	fun
mother of the bride	ugly
mother of the groom	glamorous
laughter	nervous
tears	happy

Part B

The wedding was last weekend. The bride looked scared and the groom kept quiet. Fortunately, the ceremony was short and the reception was long and lots of fun. Although the weather was hot, the ugly mother of the bride wore a long-sleeved wool dress that barely fit her. The mother of the groom, on the other hand, was very glamorous. She acted like the star of the whole show. There was a lot of nervous laughter at the reception. Some people didn't know how long the marriage would last. When the couple left for their honeymoon, tears of happiness streamed down the cheeks of the bride's mother.

———— Working Out ————   page 43

2. Trisha's New Year's Eve party was wild.

3. It makes no difference.

4. You can be sure of that!

5. Tom is so crabby that we're all being very careful not to upset him.

6. Her new dress is very unusual.

7. I didn't want us to get involved in a serious conversation.

8. Tell me the truth and don't try to trick me.

———— Working Out ————   page 45

To whom it may concern:

I am writing to you about the enclosed bills.

In October and November, I sent letters informing you that I want to cancel my subscription to the Atlas Record of the Month Club. As of today, I am still receiving records. I have been mailing back these records for two months.

I should not be charged for records sent to me after I canceled my subscription. I should bill you for the postage it took to return the records each month.

Please stop all shipments of records and all billing.

Thank you!

Section II Answers

Chapter 5
Adding Information to Sentences

page 51 ———————————— **Working Out** ————————————

The party was great. Dean and his wife Virginia were there. It was good to see them. Lauren and Betty were guests. They asked how you were.

Our new chair and desk look great. Mark and I are enjoying the new place. You and Mom should come and see it.

pages 52-53 ———————————— **Working Out** ————————————

Your answers will be different from these. Make sure you changed singular words to plural words when necessary.

2. A person I really admire is my sister.
   Another person I really admire is Betty Ford.
   People I really admire are my sister and Betty Ford.

3. For dinner today, I had steak.
   I also had potatoes for dinner today.
   I had steak and potatoes for dinner today.

4. One of my least favorite activities is getting up in the morning.
   Another one of my least favorite activities is taking out the garbage.
   Two of my least favorite activities are getting up in the morning and taking out the garbage.

5. I hate a song that is sung by Van Halen.
   The song is also sung by Roy Orbison.
   I hate a song that is sung by Van Halen and Roy Orbison.

6. My closest friend is a taxi driver.
   She is also a mother of three.
   My closest friend is a taxi driver and a mother of three.

Working Out
pages 55-56

2. To apply for citizenship, a person must turn in a petition, a fingerprint card, and three photographs of himself.

3. Husbands, wives, and children must apply separately.

4. There are two witnesses, an applicant, and an examiner at a citizenship test.

5. At the final hearing there is a judge, an applicant, and an examiner.

6. Applicants for citizenship have to make it through a petition, a test, a final hearing, and a loyalty oath.

7. My grandparents, my aunt, and my uncle are naturalized citizens.

8. My brother, my sister, and I saw each of them declared citizens.

Working Out
pages 58-59

Danny always passed, ran, and kicked better than any other kid. Now he plays quarterback and runs track at the local high school. I still coach and encourage him. I remember and still tell people about one game in particular. Danny hustled, passed, and ran his heart out. He is working and planning on becoming an All-American someday. I scrimp and save to send him to college.

Working Out
pages 61-63

Part A

2. Mr. Sanchez always reads labels on cans at the grocery store.

3. People should watch their fat intake carefully when dieting.

4. Ed Lavin always buys a new car from a well-known dealership during midseason sales.

5. Julie likes to compare prices at various stores before buying anything.

6. Mrs. Bing has a life insurance policy in a safe deposit box at the bank.

Part B

Of course, your answers will be different. Did you combine "when," "where," and "how" words like the models below do?

2. The income tax forms sat untouched on the table for three weeks.

3. She looked longingly at the tray of desserts in the cafe last night.

4. The thief quickly left the apartment on Broadway at 3:00 P.M. today.

5. He answered the question on the test slowly at the last minute.

6. The window on the third floor opened easily today.

pages 65-67

Working Out

Part A

You could have written many different kinds of descriptions of the picture. Check your sentences to see if any more ideas could be combined. Do you have enough variety in your sentences?

Part B

You may have combined some ideas in different ways. That's OK. Compare your work to the description below. See if you could combine more ideas into one sentence.

I was stacking old magazines in my uncle's basement. Suddenly I noticed something strange. It was a huge captain's trunk. I pushed, pulled, and finally turned the trunk around. Inside was an Indian blanket, some pottery, and a long rolled-up paper.

I spread the paper on the floor. It was a drawing of an old Indian couple on a wooden porch. Their faces stared back at me. The man's face was lined and wrinkled. He was frowning and staring straight ahead. The woman's face was softer, less wrinkled, and more cheerful.

They wore work clothes. The man's overalls were baggy and too long for him. He wore a belt, a work shirt, and a bandana. He had a cowboy hat on his head. In his hand, he held a tobacco pouch. The woman wore a long dress and an apron. The wind had blown her apron. She was holding it down with her hands. The woman's dress was hooked with safety pins. She wore a cap, earrings, and laced boots.

There was a screen door, a window, and two signs behind the couple. They must have been standing in front of a store or trading post.

Who could have drawn this picture? It was a mystery. I took it home, framed it, and sold it to an art gallery.

Chapter 6
Combining Sentences to Describe

─────────────── **Working Out** ───────────────

2. There are openings busing dishes, **and** jobs pumping gas aren't hard to find.

3. There are eleven restaurants in town, **and** three service stations are open all night.

4. **Both** busing dishes **and** pumping gas require little experience.

5. The restaurant job requires only filling out an application, **and** the gas station job requires only a short interview.

6. **Both** the restaurant job **and** the gas station job have suitable hours.

─────────────── **Working Out** ─────────────── pages 73-74

2. Things were different back when I was young; **however,** I still think we were ahead of our time.

3. Our generation had certain commitments, **but** this generation seems to have different ones.

4. We made progress with civil rights, **but** people now seem concerned about other things.

5. Many of us are veterans of Viet Nam; **however,** many of us fought against that war.

6. In the sixties, social action was important, **yet** today people seem to think only of themselves.

7. Hippies gave away flowers, **but** today punk rockers wear razor blades and spikes.

8. In our day, songs had messages, **but** today's songs are too commerical.

9. We wanted people to be positive; **however,** people became more negative over the years.

10. I don't want to live in the past, **but** I sure do miss the 1960s.

─────────────── **Working Out** ─────────────── page 77

2. Barry Friedman, an insurance salesman, wrote the story.

3. Barry and his wife, a hairstylist, met through Intermingle.

4. Intermingle, a modern service, videotapes its clients.

5. From the tape, his wife, a very outgoing person, thought he was smooth and confident.

6. Later, Barry, an honest man, confessed that he was really shy.

7. His date, also an honest person, eventually married him anyway.

pages 79-80 ——————————————— **Working Out** ———————————————

2. Harry, who is a friend of mine, talked me into going with him.

3. His brother, who thinks he knows everything, didn't want to go.

4. I signed up for the GED class, which is held in the evenings.

5. Ron May, who knew Harry, signed me up for it.

6. I now have my high school diploma, which means a lot to me.

7. Now I'm taking their accounting class, which is offered only once a year.

8. Harry, who always signs up for something, is taking a graphic arts class.

9. These adults, who are eager to learn, can benefit by taking night classes.

10. I have made many new friends, who feel as I do about Lakeside.

page 83 ——————————————— **Working Out** ———————————————

2. After her husband had retired, Estelle wanted a job that would provide extra money.

3. A newspaper that had "part-time help wanted" ads was all she needed.

4. The bus that she took to her first interview was late.

5. The home that she would clean was in a friendly neighborhood.

6. Estelle was hired by the husband and wife that interviewed her.

7. She organized an entire household that really needed her.

pages 85-86 ——————————————— **Working Out** ———————————————

2. **Before** I get there, I'm already tired from sorting and packing clothes.

3. **When** I arrive, the attendant starts giving me a hard time.

4. **As** I'm getting change, she's complaining that I'm using too many machines.

5. **While** I pour the soap in, I wish for a new washing machine.

6. **After** my old one broke, I had to go to the Biltmore Avenue Laundromat.

7. **When** the washer stops, I have to fight for a dryer.

8. **As** I jump over a laundry cart, the clothes I carry drip on the floor.

9. **While** the attendant mops up after me, she complains about the mess I make.

10. **After** my clothes are dry, I fold them and get out of there.

--- **Working Out** ---

pages 88-89

You may have combined fewer sentences. You may also have combined some in different ways. This is ok. Compare your work to the paragraphs below and decide if you could improve your writing at all.

> My brothers are a little hard to describe. Cal is much older than I am, but Brian is younger. You can tell a lot about them from the cars they drive. Cal, a family man, drives a station wagon. The car, which is called a ranch wagon, is not a new model at all. Often, there are toys on the floor of the car, and the seats are sticky from the children's spilling soda pop.
>
> Cal's family comes before his car; however, Brian loves his car more than anything. Brian, the swinging single of the family, owns a very classy car. His car is a classic British model that has a steering wheel on the right, not the left.
>
> Cal wants things to be practical, but Brian wants things to be impressive. Both Cal and Brian know quality when they see it. Most people admire Brian's car, yet Cal thinks it is too showy.
>
> Both Brian and Cal wanted to live far from the city. Brian, who was determined to have the best of everything, found a country home in an exclusive suburb. Cal, who was determined to care for his family, moved to a quiet little town.

Chapter 7
Relating Ideas to Persuade or Explain

--- **Working Out** ---

pages 94-95

Remember that you may have used a different connecting word (either *since* or *because*) to combine the sentences. You also may have used a different order. That's OK. Make sure you used the correct punctuation and that you always attached *since* or *because* to the reason.

2. Our neighborhood is neither pretty nor safe **because** the streets and sidewalks are covered with litter.

3. **Since** there is a lot of work to be done here, we need as many people as possible to help out.

4. Everyone should participate in a cleanup day **since** everyone will benefit from a cleaner place to live.

5. We are planning to divide into two different groups **because** the work will go more smoothly that way.

6. **Since** weekends are most convenient for everyone involved, Saturday and Sunday will be Neighborhood Cleanup Days.

pages 97-98 ——————————————— **Working Out** ———————————————

Again, you may have chosen a different connecting word from the one in some of the sentences below. That's OK. You are the writer, and it is your choice. These are meant only as models for you to check your work against.

2. The Alliance of the Disabled was not pleased with the present transportation system; **therefore**, it planned to insist on a new bus route for the disabled.

3. The alliance is a very well-known lobby group, **so** its presentation got plenty of media coverage.

4. **Because** the alliance speeches were clear and forceful, the Transportation Board listened carefully.

5. Getting on and off regular buses is a problem for these people; **therefore**, special service is needed for them to get around.

6. The disabled have an equal right to public services, **so** without special buses, their rights are being denied.

7. Cutbacks were needed to make ends meet **because** the board said that city tax revenues were down.

8. Finally, the mayor decided that the rights of the disabled were most important; **therefore**, the new bus service was approved.

page 101 ——————————————— **Working Out** ———————————————

Of course, your sentences will be different from those below. Just use these models to compare with your work.

2. Addison broke his arm in the car accident; **moreover**, he fractured his collar bone.

3. I usually spend my evenings at the local hangout; **furthermore**, I spend many days there.

4. A skill I really found valuable to learn is using a calculator; **moreover**, it is a skill I really enjoy.

5. My goals in life sometimes seem impossible; **furthermore**, the list of them seems to get longer and longer.

6. One thing that really drives me crazy is a dirty kitchen; **furthermore**, I really can't stand dirty bathrooms.

page 103 ——————————————— **Working Out** ———————————————

Since your ideas will be different, just use these sentences as models. Make sure you used the correct punctuation in your work.

2. Mrs. Dantis will keep gaining more and more weight **if** she doesn't stop eating all those doughnuts and ice cream bars.

3. **If** I read more of the newspaper, I will learn more about the world and its people.

4. **If** you keep yelling at me like that, I will have to hit you.

5. I'm going to buy a new tent **if** I can put away enough money this month.

6. **If** I wear a lampshade on my head, people will think I'm very funny.

---------------- **Working Out** ---------------- page 105

Parts A and B

These sentences are written in two ways: one with the connecting word first in the sentence and one with the connecting word in the middle. This is done to show the variety of sentences you can write without changing meaning.

1. Seth bought a new tie **though** he had no need for one.
   Though he had no need for one, Seth bought a new tie.

2. We chose a new insurance plan **although** we liked the old one.
   Although we liked the old one, we chose a new insurance plan.

3. The band played on Thursday **although** they were scheduled for Friday.
   Although they were scheduled for Friday, the band played on Thursday.

4. Sometimes people can't sleep **though** they are tired and run-down.
   Though they are tired and run-down, sometimes people can't sleep.

5. Capital punishment is fair **though** it is taking another's life.
   Though it is taking another's life, capital punishment is fair.

6. We should elect Mrs. Lloyd **although** she has little experience.
   Although she has little experience, we should elect Mrs. Lloyd.

---------------- **Working Out** ---------------- page 107

Remember that there are lots of different ways to combine the sentences in this letter. Just because your sentences are different, they are not necessarily wrong. Be sure you used a joining word that makes sense and that you used commas and semicolons where needed.

The Statue of Liberty needs a lot of repair, **so** many people from across the country are donating money. Some citizens of Baytown do not want to help pay for the repair **although** they agree that the statue is a mess.

These citizens feel that only New York benefits from the statue **because** it is a tourist attraction there. **Since** New Yorkers enjoy the statue, they should pay for its repair. The citizens of New York let the statue decay in the first place; **moreover,** they did nothing about it for years.

Although I respect the people of Baytown, I disagree with them. The Statue of Liberty was a gift to all Americans; **therefore,** we are all responsible for it. **If** we continue to let it fall apart, other countries will think we have lost our pride as a nation.

Though extra money is scarce these days, we can all donate to this worthy cause. **If** we restore our national symbol, we can be proud of our country.

Chapter 8
Writing for a Purpose

page 111 ——————————————— **Working Out** ———————————————

Your article may look different from this one because you may have chosen different ways to combine sentences. Does yours have good variety like the article below, and are all your sentences written correctly?

> The sold-out Tower Theater in Philadelphia was the scene of an old time rock and roll party. It was February 13, a Saturday night, and people had come to hear the British soul of Wham! Wham!, the latest musical import from Great Britain, features two talented young men. These handsome men, George Michael and Andrew Ridgeley, gave the audience ninety minutes of song and entertainment. The audience got 100% Wham! all night. Wham! wanted its first American tour to be special and exciting. The band chose to play only in medium-size concert halls, which people filled every time. The Tower Theater, which has a long history of rock and soul, was a perfect place to stop.

pages 114-15 ——————————————— **Working Out** ———————————————

1. I became an assistant district attorney, **and** I put my share of criminals behind bars.

2. **If** you obey the law, you should be protected.

3. **When** I first ran for Congress, all the political experts said a Democrat could not win in my home district of Queens.

4. We are going to win **because** Americans across this country believe in the same basic dream.

5. **If** we can do this, we can do <u>anything</u>.

6. **Because** our own faith is strong, we will fight to preserve the freedom of faith for others.

7. Let no one doubt that we will defend America's security **and the cause of freedom** around the world.

8. **If** we leave our children nothing else, let us leave them this earth as we found it—whole and green and full of life.

page 117 ——————————————— **Working Out** ———————————————

1. There was no one to help him, **so** he pulled the boat up as far as he could.

2. His left hand was still cramped, **but** he was unknotting it slowly.

3. The sun was hot now **although** the breeze was rising gently.

4. He knew quite well the pattern of what could happen **when** he reached the inner part of the current.

5. The fish had slowed again **and** was going at its usual pace.

6. The sun had gone down **while** he had been in the fight with the sharks.

——————— Working Out ———————

pages 120-21

1. The repeated phrase in this passage is *I have a dream*. This repetition is effective because it emphasizes what the writer and speaker feels is important. Do you notice a strong rhythm when you read through Dr. King's words?

2. The sentence "I have a dream that one day even the state of Mississippi, a state sweltering with the heat of injustice, sweltering with the heat of oppression, will be transformed into an oasis of freedom and justice" uses an appositive to describe Mississippi. Can you see the appositive set off by commas, which you learned about in Chapter 5?

    Here are two sentences that could be combined to make this one:

    a. I have a dream that one day the state of Mississippi will be transformed into an oasis of freedom and justice.

    b. Mississippi is a state sweltering with the heat of injustice, sweltering with the heat of oppression.

3. Here are a couple of examples of sentences you may have written:

    I have a dream that my children will one day live in a nation where they will not be judged by what their parents do for a living but by what they themselves can accomplish.

                                    OR

    I have a dream that my children will one day live in a nation where they will not be judged by how much money they earn but by how much good they bring to the world.

4. *WHAT HE HAS:* a dream

    REASON NOT TO: we face the difficulties of today and tomorrow

Section III Answers

Chapter 9
Editing Your Work

page 127 ———— **Working Out** ————

    The Comunity Youth Center have started its own Little League *(Community / has / its)*

team! The team is for boys and girls 9-12 years of age Living in

the Mercino Park area. Players will be selected on a first come/

first served basis but if enough youngsters apply, a second team

will be formed.

    The Community Council and Coach Pat Stern is handling *(are)*

applications. The child must be healthy, available for practice, and

has to be able to get along with other kids Equipment will be *(and uniforms)*

supplied by the center. Uniforms too.

    Some games will be played across town. Pat Stern and me will *(I)*

take the team to these games in the center's bus. Pat a former junior high coach is the perfect chaperone.

Register on Saturday morning, 12:00 until 3:00, in the lobby of the center. *Practice* practice begins the following Saturday at 8:30.

───────── **Working Out** ───────── `page 129`

Dear Mr. Craft:

I live in your Woodstock Building. On 52nd Street. Mr. Ronnie Counts is our building manager. Mr. Counts has informed me that my rent is more than five days overdue. He said I could be evicted. If I don't pay within two weeks.

I don't believe I should be harassed. By Mr. Counts. I have never been late before. *I* Did tell him ahead of time about this month. You see, I changed jobs. My other employer paid me every two weeks. No final check *has arrived* from him yet. My new employer pays me once a month on the fifteenth. I have not received my first check from him yet. Because I am a new employee.

I explained this to Mr. Counts. I will pay my rent. As soon as I can. Would you tell Mr. Counts not to harass me unnecessarily? Thank you.

Sincerely,

Sylvia Levine

───────── **Working Out** ───────── `page 131`

I never would have bought a CB radio for myself, *but* Harry said I needed one. We had just moved out to the country, I had to drive forty miles to work. The drive was miles of woods and cornfields, and Harry was worried something might happen. At first I was shy about the CB, *so* I hardly used it. My handle was "Buttercup," *but* that didn't sound tough enough. I got into the habit of listening to truck drivers. From them, I got to know all the speed traps. I enjoyed their slang and secret messages. I never radioed any of them, *because* I couldn't think of anything to say. One cold winter night I was on my way home from work. I heard a noise *,and* the car went out of control. I *when* got control I found myself in a ditch on the side of the road. My CB

was still working, I radioed for help. Finally a trucker's voice came
over the radio ∧ he asked me where I was. I told him, and he said he
would radio for a tow truck. I was saved!

[margin note above "working, I": so]
[margin note above "radio": HE]

Chapter 10
Everything in Its Place

page 135 ———————————— **Working Out** ————————————

Dear Mr. Brooks:

I hear that Ivan Petrovich and his wife have applied for an
apartment in our building. My wife Rosa and me~~me~~ *I* have known them
for years. We met Olga and he~~he~~ *him* shortly after they came to the
United States. We have been fast friends ever since.

They were also the best neighbors we ever had. Ivan and me~~me~~ *I*
work at the same factory. Olga and him~~him~~ *he* both have steady jobs and
are never late with the rent. They even helped Rosa and~~X~~ *me* when I
was out of work.

Bob, I would appreciate it if you would do this favor for Rosa
and~~X~~ *me*. Please approve the Petroviches' application. You won't
regret it.

Sincerely,

Miguel Solis

page 137 ———————————— **Working Out** ————————————

February 19, 1985

Dear Aunt Benita,

It has been an a~~w~~ful *awfully* long time since we've seen you. We hope
you are well and re~~al~~ *really* happy in your new apartment.

Our daughter Molly is five now. She is a good girl and plays
qui~~et~~ *quietly* in the yard by herself. However, she can be bad sometimes.
Yesterday I heard a sudden, lou~~dly~~ *loud* crash. I quickly ran to the
kitchen. I couldn't see Molly anywhere.

I went to the back door and ~~eager~~ _eagerly_ looked about the yard.

There she was, under the kitchen window, ~~loud~~ _loudly_ banging together

two garbage can covers. "Was I being bad?" she asked with a

twinkle in her eye. I just had to laugh at her little joke.

Anyway, expect to see us at the family reunion this summer.

We won't miss you so ~~terrible~~ _terribly_ if we have something to look

forward to.

Your niece,

Gwen

───────────── **Working Out** ─────────────   page 139

Dear Senator Waters:

I am writing to give testimony (that would ensure funding for)

alternative schools (in support of Senate Bill HB 2437).

I dropped
After ~~dropping~~ out of high school, things went from bad to

I didn't finish
worse. Because of ~~not finishing~~ high school, the world of work had

no place for me. I was the last hired and the first fired. I could get

Not
jobs that paid only minimum wage. (I fought with my bosses) ~~not~~

knowing how to behave. x

I decided that
Wanting to get my act together, Monroe Alternative School was

the place for me. I finished my high school education and took job

orientation classes. I didn't have to worry about fitting in. I am now

and am
enrolled in a first-rate technical school setting my sights on a

career in computer programming.

Dropouts have rights too. They have the right to a second

chance. Second chances are cheaper than long unemployment

lines. Please vote for HB 24371.

Sincerely,

Jeffrey Wilkins

Chapter 11
Everything Must Match

page 143

———————————————— **Working Out** ————————————————

News reports about Congress h~~as~~ *have* been a big disappointment

this year. Congressional trips to Europe and the Far East ~~is~~ *are* always

being discussed. Who is paying for these trips? The IRS or the

Government Accounting Office ha~~ve~~ *has* to investigate these trips for

the sake of American taxpayers.

The Senate and the House vo~~tes~~ *vote* too much with the President

these days. The branches of government ~~is~~ *are* supposed to provide

checks and balances against each other. So why d~~o~~ *does* the President

keep getting his MX missiles? Congress nee~~d~~ *needs* to work harder to

stop the arms race. It needs to provide a veto of the farm bill too.

Many Congressmen were not even around for the vote. They were

away on "business trips."

A new President or new members of Congress ~~is~~ *are* needed to

keep the public interest in mind. The votes of all citizens ~~is~~ *are* needed

to make sure this happens.

page 145

———————————————— **Working Out** ————————————————

TO: Mr. Henry A. Goodson, Vice President

Each of us in the clerical pool wants th~~eir~~ *her* children in a day

care center in the vicinity. Some of us travel for miles before and

after work to pick up h~~er~~ *our* children at nursery schools or baby-

sitters' homes.

We regularly have to refuse overtime. Everyone of the clerks

has gotten into trouble with th~~eir~~ *her* supervisor for lateness. Mr. Svec

was reported to have mentioned several of us in th~~eir~~ *his* monthly

report.

Many of our major companies today run ~~its~~ their own day care

centers. These centers are very profitable. Convenience and peace

of mind have ~~its~~ their benefits. Contented employees work harder. They

also come in earlier and accept overtime.

Please look into this matter. Either we or our supervisor wants

to get together with you about it soon.

─────────── **Working Out** ───────────   pages 148-49

Part A

2. Tim didn't know whether to listen
    to the radio, **watch** the television,
    or play the stereo.

3. The restaurant serves pancakes,
    hamburgers, and omelets.

4. Raoul's girlfriend is kind,
    affectionate, and **patient**.

5. Stephanie opened the door slowly,
    carefully, and **fearfully**.

Part B

Our new day camp will be fun, exciting, and ~~can be enjoyed~~ enjoyable.

The children will need a vacation from school, and you will need to

vacation from them.

This year the kids will enjoy hiking, swimming, singing, and ~~do~~ doing

arts and crafts. You will get some free time and ~~be having~~ have peace

of mind.

Contact Mindy for information about registration at 532-1616.

Chapter 12
Problems with Punctuation

page 153 ─────────────── **Working Out** ───────────────

From the desk of

Kim Pyun

Your
~~You're~~ letter of resignation caught me by surprise. It's ~~I's~~ always a

difficult thing to lose a good employee. This is especially true with

whose
someone ~~who's~~ work has been as good as yours.

you're
~~Your~~ welcome to come by the office before you leave. I hear

your   They're
~~you're~~ men are giving you a going-away party. ~~Their~~ going to miss

their
you. You've been ~~they're~~ supervisor for a number of years now.

Good luck at Beckwith Brothers in California. It's ~~I's~~ a great

you're
company, and ~~your~~ going to love the climate.

page 155 ─────────────── **Working Out** ───────────────

Dear Mr. O'Geara:

Winter is over, and it is time to start repairing potholes. My

neighbor, who is a clerk in the records department, told me an

interesting fact. Although, our neighborhood draws some tourist

trade, our streets have been repaired only three times.

Because the potholes are now quite big, I suggest you get your

workers, over here soon. The streets, have flooded badly this

spring, so you may need to work, on the sewers as well.

Our block club will be having a meeting, on Sunday. You are

invited to come. We are really very angry about the condition of our

streets; moreover, we intend to write the mayor.

Sincerely,

Roberto Duff

Working Out

page 158

On Tuesday evening, March 24, 1986 we will be offering a free health education lecture. Our guest speaker, back by popular demand, will be Dr. Helen Fairchild Curreros.

The lecture will be held at the City-Wide Adult Education Center, 1411 West Fourth Street, Houston, Texas 41173. By the way, you can write to the center for further information and a list of future programs.

Ladies, it's important that you and your loved ones attend this lecture. Dr. Curreros will be discussing the seven warning signs of cancer. Moreover, she will discuss how fear is cancer's best friend.

                              East Texas Women's Society